PLACE IN RETURN BOX to remove this checkout from your record.
TO AVOID FINES return on or before date due.

DATE DUE	DATE DUE	DATE DUE
JAN 0 9 2006	0 5	

Islam and the Modern Age

ISLAM
and the
MODERN AGE

An Analysis and an Appraisal

by

ILSE LICHTENSTADTER

With a Foreword by
SIR MUHAMMAD ZAFRULLA KHAN
Vice-President, International Court of Justice

BOOKMAN ASSOCIATES
New York

DEDICATED IN SINCERE FRIENDSHIP

TO

DR. M. RAZIUDDIN SIDDIQI

VICE-CHANCELLOR

PESHAWAR UNIVERSITY, PAKISTAN

Printed in the U.S.A.

NOBLE OFFSET PRINTERS, INC.

NEW YORK 3, N.Y.

Foreword

Dr. Lichtenstadter has lived on intimate terms with Muslims in their homelands, including Egypt and Pakistan. She has thus had valuable opportunities to observe their habits and modes of life, but also to study their weaknesses, failings and shortcomings. She experienced, too, the courtesy, graciousness and hospitality extended to an honoured guest whose sympathy and understanding had made her one of them. She is, therefore, in a position to appraise the problems and perplexities that confront Muslims at the opening of the atomic age.

Dr. Lichtenstadter sets out some of these problems and difficulties in the second part of her valuable study. She also draws attention to certain lines of approach which, in her view, should prove helpful in resolving some, if not all, of these difficulties.

Muslim intelligentsia will not question the validity and urgency of the principal step urged by Dr. Lichtenstadter, namely, "the re-opening of the door of free interpretation." Indeed, this door should never have been deemed closed. Human society is dynamic; the need of guidance, both by formulation of principle and by regulation of conduct, is constant. To declare the "door of interpretation" sealed is to force a rift between the ever-growing need for change and the static guidance, which must, in time, widen into a gulf too broad to be bridged. The result would be frustration, confusion and chaos.

Fortunately, Islam is not in so desperate a situation. At no time in its history has the entire body of divines and jurists subscribed to that theory. The Koran clearly and repeatedly announces that it will at all times continue to yield guidance.

In this context, another point, referred to incidentally by Dr. Lichtenstadter, needs prior elucidation, namely, the prob-

lem of contradictions in the Koran. There are none; indeed
the Koran itself repudiates that allegation. Alleged contradictions are merely the result of neglect of canons of interpretation and unfamiliarity with Koranic idiom. Equally, no part
of the Koran was abrogated by any other. This notion resulted
from a misinterpretation of the word *Âyah* in the verse "Whatever *âyah* (sign) We abrogate or cause to be forgotten, We bring
one better than that or the like thereof" (Sûrah 2, verse 100).
The context shows that it is not abrogation of any verse (*âyah*)
of the Koran that is implied. For not a single one was ever
excluded from the Koranic text as having been abrogated. To
assume that both the abrogated and the abrogating verses were
found in it would certainly lead to contradiction, a possibility
repudiated by the Holy Book.

This verse and related ones clearly try to answer the question
"What purpose is the Koran designed to serve, considering that
it affirms the truth of previously revealed scriptures?" Part of
the guidance contained in previous revelations was limited in
its application to a particular stage in the development of the
peoples to whom they were addressed. Having served their
purpose, their guidance became out-of-date; it was abrogated by
the Koran and a better one, suited to the needs of all mankind
throughout the ages, revealed in it. True guidance in earlier
revelations that had been forgotten or overlooked was revived
in the Koran. The rest is common to all revelations and was
confirmed in it.

To revert to the theme of "free interpretation" of the
Koran with reference to new problems arising in human society,
it is axiomatic that such interpretation must keep pace with
changes in the pattern of human life and thought. It is necessary to keep in mind the unique character of the Koran which
is not yet fully appreciated even by those Western scholars
who have come closest to the spirit of Islam in their study and
research. The Koran is not, as they assume, the product of the
mind and intellect of the Prophet. It is the record of verbal
revelations vouchsafed by God to the Prophet over a period of
twenty-three years. This claim is not accepted by non-Muslims.
But unless it is constantly kept in mind, it is not possible to

appreciate the manner in which the problem dwelt upon by
Dr. Lichtenstadter and other scholars may receive a solution.
If that claim were not true and well-founded, the whole structure
of Islam would be based upon a precarious foundation and
would collapse. If, however, the Koran is the very word of God,
then it is *alive,* as the universe is alive, and it is in a sense a
universe in itself. Then it shares with the universe a dynamic
quality that would enable it to keep pace with the changing
pattern of human life and society.

The Koran itself states (in Sûrah 3, verse 5) that certain
verses are decisive in meaning and the basis of the Book, but
that there are others that are susceptible of different interpretations. These must be interpreted with reference and in
subordination to the decisive ones. Guidance in changing conditions of human life would be afforded through interpretation
by "those who are firmly grounded in knowledge" or by God
Himself Who would illumine and set forth the meaning of the
guidance contained in the Koran through revelation.

The solution of the principal difficulty mentioned by Dr.
Lichtenstadter will therefore be found in the Koran. It draws
repeated attention to the phenomena of nature as a basis for
the understanding of spiritual truths and exhorts to study
nature and its laws for the progress and enrichment of human
life. It will certainly not prove inadequate merely because the
human mind is beginning to discover more and more of the
laws governing the forces of nature. The recent rapid advance
in the fields of science and technology has given greater knowledge and power to man. This in itself is not a matter for anxiety
or fear. The troubling question is whether man's moral and
spiritual resources will enable him to employ this new knowledge and power for the benefit of his fellow beings and not for
their destruction. This problem confronts not merely the Muslims, but all those who base the regulation of human life on
faith and divine guidance. Those who have, in this generation,
undertaken a fresh study of the Koran are confident that its
guidance is more than adequate for its solution.

Dr. Lichtenstadter's study of contemporary Muslim society
reveals a degree of understanding and sympathy that will be

much appreciated by her Muslim and non-Muslim readers alike. Her book should prove of great value in promoting better understanding between the Muslims and the West, so sorely needed in our time. Muslim readers will be enabled to see many of the problems facing them through the eyes of one who has expounded them not for the sake of criticism but in the hope of better understanding and as a help toward their solution.

ZAFRULLA KHAN

Preface

This book is an attempt to analyse the problems of the contemporary Muslim world in relation to their ancient foundations and to examine the reasons for their pre-eminence in our day. Those factors in Islam that remain valid independent of external circumstances or specific epochs are to be brought into relief, for they provide the unchanging inner motivation for Muslim action and thought.

The Islamic world has emerged from its centuries-long isolation and has renewed its participation in world affairs. Many of its conflicts are caused by the re-established contact with the West; their effects on Muslim attitudes, as well as their solutions, gravely concern both East and West. The second task of this essay, therefore, is an analysis of the problems caused by the meeting of the western and eastern mentalities.

The first part of the book, which deals with Islamic principles, utilizes literary sources, mainly the original Muslim classics, while the second part is based extensively on the author's personal observations. The study aims at an integrated representation of the problems that have faced Islam throughout the nearly fourteen centuries of its existence, not at a descriptive enumeration of detail. This purpose also accounts for a certain selectivity in the topics discussed.

Three extensive stays in Egypt (in 1947, 1950/51, and 1955) and one in West Pakistan (in 1955), with short visits to other Arab and Middle East countries (including three weeks in Delhi, India, and its surroundings), profoundly impressed the writer. They provided, through personal observation and friendship with men and women in every walk of life, the opportunity to experience "the Muslim way of life" and evaluate the Muslim's point of view. Her hosts welcomed their Jewish guest and made her feel at home in their midst in spite of the difference in the forms of their life and their religion. Her friends in Egypt and Pakistan freely revealed to her their struggle and their faith. Often they were outspoken in their criticism of western ways and the lack of western understanding of theirs. Yet, in spite of some defiance, the deep conflict in the eastern mind between the wish to follow the example of the West and the desire to retain traditional values was always evident.

As an Islamist and Arabist, the author's study and primary interest are devoted to the religion, culture, literature and history of the Arabs and the Muslim world. But in order to understand Islam deeply and correctly, the sociological, economic and cultural-anthropological aspects had to be observed and taken into account. However, the writer evaluates her material as an Islamist, analysing the observed trends as forces in the development of Islam in the modern world, as religious conflicts and their attempted solution.

The author is trying to write *sine ira et studio*, to give the Muslim point of view and discuss debatable and polemical problems without bias in favour or against them. She endeavours to clarify the Muslim stand over against that of the West. She is not writing as an apologist for, but as an impartial student of, Islam; nor is she pleading any special cause or currying favour with any side, but only aspires to honesty in her interpretations. She may therefore not always please the Muslim or the Western reader; but scholarship, and her deep friendship for Muslims and respect for their faith, compel her to state the truth according to her best judgement and ability.

The book was nearly finished when the Suez Canal crisis broke out. The last few pages had been drafted before the invasion of Egypt shocked the conscience of the world. However, these agonizing events did not invalidate any part of this essay. On the contrary, they only gave added weight to the author's conviction that more penetrating comprehension of the well-springs of Islamic culture is needed to understand the conflicts and mutual attraction or repulsion between East and West.

It is too early to evaluate that crisis in all its ramifications and conflicting causes. In the public debate, the political and economic factors, the emotions of opposing nationalisms and the background contest of great powers overshadow its real implications. In the rivalries and recurrent outbreaks of strife and in the wide-spread unrest of our time the historian might see phases in an epochal change comparable to that of the most decisive periods in history, such as the decline of the Roman Empire or the centuries of the Reformation and the French Revolution. More specifically, the crisis in the Middle East is part of the struggle for supremacy between Asia and the West, to this writer the decisive issue of our era. The conflict between Israel and the Arabs must be judged and eventually settled in this larger context.

There remains for the author the pleasant duty of thanking those who contributed to her progress. First and foremost, her gratitude is due to the Social Science Research Council which twice (in 1950 and 1955) awarded her its Grant-in-Aid for Research to finance her field work in Egypt and in Pakistan. Next she wishes to record the encouragement received from her dear Mother and from her friends among the Orientalists. They are too numerous to be mentioned individually; let therefore the names of Professors T. H. Gaster, G. E. von Grunebaum, P. K. Hitti, G. Levi Della Vida, K. H. Menges, A. U. Pope, and F. Rosenthal stand for all.

In Egypt, her friends are numerous; Mme Wafiyah Izzi Ayyad, Professors Ibrahim al-Ibyari and Muhammad Mustafa may be singled out, as being closest to her. The author recalls with gratitude the courtesies received from Dr. M. Husain Heikal whose recent death she greatly laments. She wishes to acknowledge, in particular, the contribution to this book made unconsciously by the inhabitants of the village in which she lived, though none of them will ever read it.

In Pakistan, too, a few friends must represent the many to whom the author is beholden. Dr. Viqar Ahmad Hamdani and Dr. Sheikh Inayatullah have been her friends since her student days. She records the graciousness of Begum Shah Nawaz,

M.L.A., as representative of that shown her by women in all the cities and villages visited. Begum Anwar G. Ahmad and other leaders of the All-Pakistan Women's Association, the American Consulate and Information Service in Karachi and Lahore, and the American and Pakistani directors and members of the Village Agriculture and Industry Development Programme in the Punjab deserve her special grateful recognition. Professor 'Abd al-Wahid of Peshawar University merits singling out, for he braved monsoon rains and all but impassable roads to take her on a tour of North West Frontier villages. The author's thanks are also due to Professor I. H. Qureshi for giving her valuable introductions. Vice-Chancellor M. R. Siddiqi's contribution to the success of her field work is acknowledged by the dedication of this essay.

In all countries visited, the author enjoyed the cooperation of government departments and their high officials. The great courtesies received from Dr. Taha Husain, then Egypt's Minister of Education, and his collaborators, are specifically acknowledged. A letter from Arthur S. Lall, Ambassador to the United Nations from India, introduced her to high-ranking members of the Indian Government who made her all-too-short stay in their country memorable. The hospitality of Professor and Mrs. M. B. Mirza and of the Muslim University at Aligarh added to the many pleasures of her travels. To all these friends, and to those not mentioned individually, but not less gratefully remembered, the author offers her sincere thanks.

In his Foreword, Sir Zafrulla Khan affords the reader an insight into the manner in which a progressive, yet conservative Muslim attempts to solve a vexing problem that from ancient times had formed the subject of a great many works by Muslim scholars. The reader will share the author's appreciation of Sir Zafrulla's contribution to this essay.

NEW YORK UNIVERSITY   I. L.

Note: In transliterating Arabic words, long vowels are indicated. For technical reasons, "diacritical signs," representing distinctive pronunciation of certain Arabic sounds, are omitted.

Contents

PROLOGUE

Gottes ist der Orient!
Gottes ist der Occident!
Nord- und südliches Gelände
Ruht im Frieden seiner Hände.

(GOETHE, *West-östlicher Diwan*)

Unto Allâh belong the East and the West, and whither-
soever ye turn, there is Allâh's countenance. Verily,
Allâh comprehends all and knows all.

(KORAN, Sûrah II, "The Cow")

PART ONE

The Problem, Its Scope and Meaning

I.

Since the nineteenth century, the western world has become increasingly aware of the impact of events in the East on its own affairs. In consequence, Westerners have ceased to regard themselves as impartial observers, mere bystanders not directly affected by the internal affairs of the East. For centuries, they had been interested only academically, or as merchants, explorers and exploiters; but developments, especially of the last half-century, have drawn East and West together in an ever closer interrelation, until at present, literally, the life of every individual, in the East as well as in the West, is affected by events in either.

Not for the first time have the two worlds come into contact with each other. The Eastern Roman Empire covered much of the territory that became the Muslim, and later, the Ottoman Empire and that is now called Near and Middle East. The cultural give and take of the Hellenistic period in that area is well documented; in the Middle Ages, they met through trade and intellectual intercourse, but also as enemies in intermittent wars that lasted for centuries. The impact of the Crusades on both western and eastern civilization is fully established, evidenced, in the West, by art and architecture, by literature, philosophy, science and commerce, in the East by the so-called Crusaders' castles and other architectural remains. For every contact, whether friendly or hostile, between different cultures, different religions, ways of life and attitudes, disseminates their underlying ideas and their respective customs, and fertilizes the thought patterns of both.

Throughout the Middle Ages and the Renaissance, this contact continued, though later not on as large a scale as in the Byzantine and Crusaders' eras. Western travellers, explorers and merchants visited many parts of Asia and the Near and Middle East and brought back knowledge of the East and a somewhat romantic love for it; often this was intermingled with contempt for the dismal state of affairs and, on the other hand, with admiration for the refinement of its arts and crafts. Frequently a burning desire to save the souls of the Asians was added. These feelings they tried to convey to those of their fellow Westerners who cared to listen.

However, this interaction was not a continuous process. There were long periods in which the West went its own way. Especially in the last century or two, it was progressing rapidly; but the East had been paralyzed for hundreds of years trapped by fettering factors in its own mental pattern as well as by external circumstances. The West regarded the East as "backward," "reactionary," uncreative, unable to follow it into the modern age. In the wake of this evaluation followed western political imperialism and the arrogant self-appraisal of its intellectual superiority.

But the East was only dormant. For centuries, its creative genius had led the medieval world in science, philosophy and the arts, even after its political decay had set in. With the rise of the Ottoman Empire, however, and its ensuing strict bureaucracy and centralized organization, it fell back and became stagnant and gradually sank into intellectual as well as political inertia. This made it easy for the western world to overpower its intellectual life just as the increasing weakness of the Ottomans made its political subjugation possible.

As a result of this conquest, contact between East and West and their mutual influence were no longer limited to a small number of isolated men who met while pursuing their individual purposes and in the process absorbed some features of their respective cultures. The political domination of whole countries resulted in a conscious effort at superimposing western organization and institutions on an entirely different, even alien, cultural pattern. But the whole rhythm of their life, their range of values, their emotional tempo and climate, their reactions to identical situations and problems were dissimilar. In consequence, the two groups lived next to each other in space, but centuries and leagues apart in spirit.

On the other hand, the close contact, even where it was only proximity in locality, of eastern and western men and women, had inevitable results. As if by osmosis, western ideas began to percolate into the eastern civilizations. Neither individuals, nor groups or institutions could escape the ever-increasing pressure of foreign rulers who introduced not only new laws and political organizations, but also social standards and religious, educational and philosophic ideas. Though often alien to the traditional pattern, these new ideas set the East wondering about its own mental attitudes and position. Sir Saiyid Ahmad Khan's (1817-1898) evaluation of this intellectual process and its inherent dangers and potentialities for Indian Islam that induced him to found the Anglo-Muslim College in Aligarh may be cited as an example.

The East looked admiringly, though often with disapproval, at the superiority of the West manifested in its political power as well as in its economic strength and technologic resourcefulness. It began to question the validity of its own institutions and sets of values. It reasoned that, to emulate these achievements, it needed only to follow the western lead in those fields. Thus began the process of "Westernization," of a conscious assimilation to western ways and modes of thought; there followed, as its outward manifestation, the adoption of western forms of behaviour, customs and ways of dress that characterized the past half century or more of eastern development and still continues to do so. The East began to take over many of the western techniques; these frequently disrupted, in the process, the delicate balance that had resulted from century-old adjustments or were unfitted to the indigenous economic and social pattern. This was paralleled by the adoption of ideological attitudes not in harmony with traditional thought or social and religious customs. The result was an intellectual and emotional upheaval that was felt eventually not only in the upper ranges of eastern society where it had begun, but that gradually penetrated into the lower tiers; it produced a feeling of restlessness and, worse, insecurity, that in the end permeated the whole eastern social organization.

Not that the attempt in itself was an unqualified evil; on the contrary, in its inevitability, it carried into our own times a factor that had been decisive in eastern and western relations throughout the ages. But while the process in the past had been organic and largely identical in East and West, propelled by fundamentally identical impulses, in the modern age, East and West started from different premises and posed dissimilar problems. Modern western thought is predominantly scientific, while the eastern mind, especially that of the Islamic East, is dominated by religion; after centuries of the most brilliant leadership in the sciences, the East had been virtually dead in that field.

The conflict in the life of the East is rooted in the discrepancy between scientific and religious thought. Science is never satisfied with its own answers and continues to search for ever more fundamental solutions to never-ending problems. Religion, on the contrary, has one answer, and one only, to all questions. For it, the existence of the Deity solves every problem once and for all; it is static, while science is dynamic. Therefore, eastern thought may be characterized as static in contrast to the dynamism of modern western thought.

It is this clash between the collective personalities of the East and the West that has produced the conflicts that our own age is called upon to solve. But no solution will be forthcoming without understanding not merely the superficial, self-evident contrasts and divergencies, but the very foundations of eastern and western thought and the roots of their different emotional or rational reactions. This duty devolves upon both groups; understanding has to be mutual in order to be effective and fruitful. It must be recognized, however, that it is equally hard for the eastern as for the western mind to abandon its own conventional directions of thought and try to fathom each other's actions and reactions. Both East and West have to discard

many preconceived ideas, wrong and hasty judgements, romantic
notions and prejudiced attitudes.

It is the strength of the East, and at the same time its
weakness, that it realizes its own shortcomings, in modern times,
in the scientific sphere which dominates modern western thought,
while at the same time it senses its superiority in the religious
and cultural field. In the latter its centuries-, even millennia-
old traditions had given a certainty, a solid, unshakable foundation to its development in all aspects of its culture, whether
political, social, religious, philosophic, and even scientific. Tragically, this certainty, this secure belief, has been undermined;
the infallibility of the answers given by the religious leaders
in accordance with tradition and century-old interpretation
has begun to be questioned. Contact with the West has shaken
faith; instead, eastern minds have become aware of the conflict between scientific evidence and religious belief, between
scientific investigation of the cosmos and religious cosmogony;
while their intellect forced them to acknowledge the correctness
of the former, their heart refused to abandon the latter. Out
of this conflict rose their endeavour to harmonize Revelation
and Science, as did the Egyptian scholar Sheikh Muhammad
'Abduh (1848-1905), an attempt that strikes the western mind
as almost tragic and may move it to pity rather than to admiration.

While these observations apply more or less to the relation
between the West and the entire world of the East, this book
will be devoted to the discussion of the specific problems posed
by the world of Islam. Though the inquiry will thus be limited
in scope, many of the implications are valid, *mutatis mutandis,*
for the whole eastern world.

II.

Islam, one of the three great monotheistic religions, has
spread far from the locality in which it originated almost fourteen hundred years ago. Though born in Arabia and at first
carried by Arabs, very soon it accepted masses of converts of
widely different racial and cultural backgrounds and origins.

In modern times, there are Muslims in Indonesia, in Egypt and in Morocco, in Russia, Central Asia and in South and Central Africa. The Iranians, the Pakistanis and the Turks are Muslims; Islam is professed in China, Cyprus and Yugoslavia. One may add that there is a number (not very large, but enough to merit mentioning) of converts to Islam of European or American origin. In the course of the centuries Islam has been able to amalgamate this variety of vastly different types into one group homogeneous at least in the religious aspect. This impressive feat has been achieved by very simple means: not, as is usually asserted, by the power of "fire and the sword," but by the strength of a religious dogma that is not too complicated to be understood by a simple and yet complex enough to satisfy the subtle mind, by virtue of a religious pattern not too difficult to uphold, and by a human attitude appealing to a great variety of men.

This diversity of racial and ethnic origins and of religious and philosophic backgrounds has been with Islam almost from its beginning. Conflicts of ideas not too dissimilar from those it faces today have therefore always confronted it. For that reason it is necessary to differentiate sharply between the Arab foundation and the Muslim development of Islam. Only at the very beginning was the Muslim almost exclusively an Arab, thus "Muslim" identical with "Arab." The task of this book is to show the evolution of the former on the fundaments of Arabian culture, to differentiate between Arabism and Islamism, to elucidate the particular, and to a certain degree ephemeral, features of Islam and its essential and eternal aspects. To anticipate conclusions: it is the latter that make Islam the great religious world force it is still today.

The original carriers of Islam, the Arabs, very soon encountered the Greek and Persian cultures, in addition to Judaism and Christianity with which already the founder of the faith had had to cope. Islam had to understand, change, incorporate and integrate their ideas into its own system or else be vanquished. Had it been defeated in this undertaking, probably not just the political history of the Near East and Europe, but, more crucial, their intellectual development would have taken an entirely different course. Out of that meeting emerged something entirely new: not a subdivision of Judaism or Christianity or Greek thought—and Islam at one time or another has been characterized as each of these—but the specific mentality, the new *Weltanschauung* that was Islam. This fact must be stressed against the strenuous efforts throughout the centuries to prove that Islam was nothing but a derivative of Judaism and Christianity, or a heretic Christian sect, and against the assertion that it was unoriginal, unimaginative, shallow and diluted in dogma, and epigonic in its philosophy. The undeniable influence of Judaism and Christianity on the development of the new faith, the obvious parallels to Bible and Gospels found in the Koran, its proven dependence on Greek thought for much of its philosophic content, do not invalidate the claim that Islam is more than an eclectic synthesis of these three. Granted, it was "creative borrowing," to use Von Grunebaum's apt phrase; but the accent was on "creative."

Mutatis mutandis, modern Islam is facing problems and conflicts not too dissimilar in character from those of the early centuries of its existence. Now, as then, it has to integrate foreign, if not utterly alien, ideas into its own system; it has the task of building states (even though the modern concept of the state differs from that of medieval times); it has to create new social institutions exacted by a new social consciousness, to make laws that are in harmony with the ancient ones yet conform to the demands of modern life. This has to be done without damaging the spirit of Islam, without demolishing its traditional framework. In its earlier centuries, Islam developed, out of sheer necessity, methods with which to meet that same challenge. These were never discarded by Islamic theology and jurisprudence, and they are therefore, for better or for worse, still the tools to be used in our age.

III.

In the course of the centuries Islam, in spite of the diversity of its components, developed into an integrated Muslim community sharply set off against other groups. It created a distinct culture, with an Islamic literature, philosophy, art and, of course, religion; any adherent of that faith, whatever his ethnic or geographic origin, could feel at home in any Muslim land and understand the ideological outlook of any other Believer. The dominance of a specific unified viewpoint also accounts for the faculty of Islam to absorb heterogeneous trends and elements of native folk-lore and superstitions without giving up its fundamental truths or losing its identity. Whenever large ethnic groups became converted to the new faith, whether during the first centuries of its existence or later, a kind of Islam congenial to their indigenous beliefs and ideas developed by the merging of native, subconsciously remembered notions with the newly accepted truths. The result of this merger was always Islam, not a sect or a new religion. The best example for this fact is Shî'î Islam which might have the greatest right to the claim of being an independent faith. Indeed, Sunnî Muslims do not shrink from denouncing Shî'ism as "idolatry." But the historical fact that is has never broken away from "official" Islam, and never in its profession of faith deviated from it except in minor phraseology, shows that it considered itself fundamentally part of Islam. The same process, though not so far-reaching in its consequences, was repeated over and over again, in India, in Indonesia, and in Africa, wherever large masses of natives were converted to the faith.

In our days, a new appraisal of Islam by its devotees is in process; the validity and adequacy of its social standards in view of the demands and preoccupations of the modern age are being scrutinized. But in all this soul searching, its fundamental truth has never been questioned. It is an undeniable fact that in the many decades, even centuries, of missionary endeavour in Islamic countries, conversions of Muslims to Christianity have been comparatively few, in some regions almost nil. Neither amongst the illiterate, poverty-stricken masses, nor amongst the intellectuals, the cultural and political leaders, has Christianity found any wide-spread entrance or acceptance. Atomic scientists, zoologists and mathematicians remain convinced Muslims. It is significant to note that there have been no conversions among the many Muslim students in western countries, however "Westernized" their outlook may have become. This is not an accident. It proves that Islam has values not only for the ignorant, but satisfies as well the religious and emotional needs of the cultured intellectual whose demands upon the scientific accuracy in the secular sphere are becoming increasingly higher.

Yet, while the validity of the religious belief, the truth of revelation, remain unaffected by this process of "Westernization," the structure of the society built upon its prescripts is scrutinized and discussed, often with a high degree of emotional heat. But before any change would be approved, religious sanction would have to be sought; this would be given only if found in the Koran itself and in the "Way (Sunnah) of the Prophet," the sources of guidance towards the right solution of all questions.

One well-known and often-discussed example is the institution of polygamy. In none of the Islamic countries, except Turkey, has polygamy been declared illegal, neither by civil nor by religious authority. It still remains a legitimate form of marriage in Egypt and Pakistan, Iran, Iraq and Syria, as well as in Indonesia. Under the influence of western attitudes and with the growing awareness of its undesirable facets, the trend towards becoming equal to the West in this most intimate sphere of life is strong; polygamy is increasingly looked upon as outmoded. Since it is practiced mainly by the lower classes, some feeling of social inferiority is sometimes attached to it. But Muslim reformers find the most valid support for monogamy in the Koran itself. The final words of the famous verse of its fourth Sûrah that allows a Muslim four wives—or rather restricts him to that number—are understood to imply that monogamy is to be preferred: "But if ye fear that ye cannot be equitable, then [marry] only one." Therefore, if Muslim religious authorities should ever be willing to agree to the outright prohibition of this traditional practice, their justification of this act would be based on the Koran itself. The holy Book is also asserted to contain many other modern concepts, that of democracy, for instance, though their meaning may be entirely different from their western connotations.

One fact emerges quite distinctly from the discussion going on in Islamic society: Islam is a vital force, not merely as a form of religious expression, but as a dynamic factor in the creation of those forms of Islamic life that the modern age demands. Any discussion of social customs must have certain basic standards by which to judge their rights or wrongs; in western society it is the Christian ethics, the Ten Commandments and the Gospels that have formed its social ideals and continue to do so. In the Muslim East, the social and religious ethics of Islam are the standard by which their development is being, and will continue to be, judged. Islam is more than a religion—it is a way of life.

PART I

THE FOUNDATIONS
OF ISLAM

CHAPTER ONE

The Cultural Foundation:
Pre-Islamic Arabian Society

I.

No culture ever developed in a vacuum. Its vitality is proved by its ability to integrate new factors into the basic beliefs and ideas that were its original core. Islam is no exception to this rule. To understand it fully, we must try to determine the various strands in its fabric, the many ideas that eventually produced the distinct entity "Islam."

Islam rose in Arabia in the early seventh century A.D. For this reason, no book dealing with that religion and the culture it created can afford to omit at least a summary of Arabia's past prior to the birth of the founder of Islam and its emergence from the Arabian Peninsula. For it was an Arab who felt singled out by Allâh to receive His Revelation to bring it to his people in their own Arabic language. Furthermore, to this day, the central, most sacred ceremony for the whole Muslim world is the annual pilgrimage to Mecca in the heart of Arabia; whoever has witnessed the celebration of the festival connected with it in any Muslim country will testify to the role it plays in the heart of every Muslim, whatever his race or nationality.

But that Arabia, into which the Prophet was born, did not come into existence only at that late time. Previous to the founding of Islam, a century-, possibly millennia-old culture and civilization had existed there which is not yet known sufficiently to evaluate it fully, either in its own right or in its importance for Muhammad and Islam. Even in ancient times, Arabia was not isolated. Despite its desolation, the paucity of its inhabitants, its forbidding climate, and the vast, uninhabited deserts, the country, largely because of its crucial location, played a role in the international relations of those times, as it does again in our own. Nor is this true only of South Arabia, the Arabia Felix of the ancient world, the importance of which in international trade and politics in the first millennium B.C. is well attested. The routes for the spice trade from India to the Mediterranean led through South Arabia, from there along the coastal areas and the oases of Central and North Arabia to Egypt or Palestine and Syria; an alternate route led through the Fertile Crescent to the Northwest. But the carriers of goods are always at the same time transmitters of ideas.

From time immemorial, Arabia was situated between eastern and western powers. Egypt and Assyria vied with each other to include South Arabia into their "sphere of influence," as is witnessed by inscriptions and pictorial representations. At one time or another, Egypt, Assyria and Iran had some sway over it, and in not too remote ages, Christianity, and even Judaism, were professed there. The powers coveted the country as a source for the valuable spices and the incense needed for their rituals; the latter is still grown in Hadramawt and customarily used in the Coptic churches in Egypt. Incense is, to this day, a favorite fumigating perfume in almost every Eastern country. Other reasons, too, made South Arabia an enviable prize. It possessed, in the millennium before Christ, a highly developed culture, well-organized states with diversified groups that had defined tasks and status in public life; irrigation systems made lucrative agriculture possible. South-Arabian civilization reached its climax in a refined architecture attested to by still-surviving temples and secular edifices in which Greek as well as Persian influence can be traced.

The pre-history of Central Arabia, on the contrary, is still entirely unknown. No excavations have been undertaken, though brilliant and courageous travellers, such as Burton, Doughty, Philby and Bertram Thomas, have explored its surface, its fauna and flora, its geography and its ethnography. In addition, in most recent years, geological research executed by mining engineers and financed by the oil interests has been carried out. Since Central Arabia was the cradle of Islam, the stage on which the whole drama unfolded, this lack of knowledge about the cultural antecedents of its Prophet is very serious. It leaves, as the tools for our understanding, nothing but derivative sources, almost exclusively literary in character and of late date and still later fixation in writing. This lack of information has led scholars and laymen alike to assert that Central Arabia had no civilization to speak of except for that of a few oases and of unsettled nomads.

But, as long as we have not explored the country with all the means of modern scholarship, no definite judgement should be made. Specifically, the rulers of Arabia still withhold permission for archaeological exploration which in other regions of the Near East has enlarged our knowledge of the ancient cultures so spectacularly. It is the writer's conviction that, once archaeological research on a large scale could be undertaken, our knowledge of the country's past might expand not only in scope but in character. For the problems under scrutiny in this study, this aspect is not of prime urgency; the picture that our literary sources give us suffices to visualize the society into which Muhammad was born and in which he grew to his later stature of Prophet.

II.

From early Islamic times, the Muslims called the centuries preceding the mission of the Prophet and the coming of Islam the "Time of Ignorance," al-Jâhilîyah. They had coined this term to distinguish the period when the unity of Allâh was proclaimed and Islam revealed from the age when the Arabs were ignorant of this great idea and steeped in error and religious darkness. Gradually, it re-acquired its ancient pre-Islamic meaning of "ignorance of any of the fine ways of life, uncivilized, crude and backward." In their desire to extol their Prophet and the new religion, the Muslims tried to erase any reminder of the pagan era, to expurge any reference to its deities, its customs, its way of life. They succeeded so well that it is difficult to restore the picture even incompletely.

Western orientalists and historians of less than a hundred years ago followed the lead of the Muslims, and it became customary to dismiss the pre-Islamic history of Central Arabia almost contemptuously as its "dark ages," devoid of civilization. Its society in the epoch before Muhammad was described as unorganized, a "community without a magistrate," as Julius Wellhausen, the renowned German orientalist (died 1919) once called it. For him, tribal society did not count as an organization. But modern cultural anthropology has taught us not to consider a society uncivilized or unorganized because it differs in form from our norms. Modern evaluation of the social structure in pagan Arabia has changed since Wellhausen's days.

However artificial the picture of Arab tribal relationships drawn by the Muslim historians and genealogies may have been, it reflects to a certain degree their actual organization, or at least the impression it conveyed to later generations. It describes a fullfledged, well-defined social organization. Within its own framework, the Arab had leadership, somewhat fluctuating, it is true; their leaders were freely elected on the strength of their character, their outstanding courage and mature judgement. Their followers willingly acknowledged this leadership and submitted to it.

Within the tribe, each individual had his secure position. As long as he was its recognized member, not an outcast or outlaw, he could expect protection, even as his co-operation and participation was expected and taken for granted. A man was born into this community and only by his own misdeeds could he lose this birthright. An outsider could be received into the tribal fold by being granted protection by one of its members; this relation was sacred and his person inviolate. Whoever attacked him did so at his risk, for his protector was honour-bound to stand up for him with all his influence and power. A slave, not connected by bonds of blood, could become affiliated to the tribe by being freed by his master or by buying his freedom from him. He would then remain within the group as the "client" *mawlà* of that family. Because of this connexion, he and his descendants forever retained membership in the tribe.

In Egyptian villages, traces of these ancient institutions may still be found. The writer was received into the community of a village under the former pattern and is still welcomed there as its member; she always felt happy and secure in person and property. Not only the people in her own village, but also the neighbouring communities respected that relation. The "client" relationship, too, is still effective. The father of one of her friends had been the slave of a leading *sheikh*, but had later been freed by his master, since the Koran commends the freeing of slaves as a meritorious deed. The freedman's son is now the trusted foreman and representative of the *sheikh's* son, and a sincere friendship unites the two men. This mirrors exactly the ancient custom; for many a *mawlà* and his descendants remained trusted agents for their former masters. Many of them became rich and were leading figures in Muslim society, whether in politics, scholarship or court life, and often instrumental, for better or worse, in the shaping of events.

The tribes combined into larger groups whenever they needed additional strength or the help of more influential ones. Thus, in the century before Muhammad, as Arab literature clearly shows, Arab society cannot be dismissed as unorganized and unstratified. Unfortunately, the narrative of our sources is disparate, their literary technique pointillistic and impressionistic; it rarely centres on a person or an event, but always stresses the detail, the incident, the anecdote. Thence the reader himself has to supply the concentration, the continuity and the evaluation, no matter whether he studies the original Arabic narrative or a translation. But if he takes that trouble, the Arab organization becomes clear in its full stratification with its clans and subtribes, each guided by a leading personality and all of them submitting to the authority of the tribal leader, the *sheikh*. Many tribal alliances gradually became permanent and known under their group appellation and all but lost their original name. The most renowned of these are the Quraish, the large group to which Muhammad's family belonged.

Remnants and echoes of tribal organization and even its counterparts can still be found in the countries of the modern Near and Middle East. The manners and customs of the Rwala Bedouins in the Syrian desert and their position in modern Syria have been investigated by the great Czech scholar Aloys Musil (born 1868). In political decisions, the Bakhtiaris and Khashghais of Iran, or the tribes of the Tribal Areas and the North-West Frontier Province in Pakistan have to be taken into serious account. The Bisharîn Bedouins, a large community of nomads, whose camp the writer visited, roam the desert from Assuan to the Red Sea and carry on considerable trade in camels and other livestock. In spite of their comparatively "uncivilized" state, they are a factor in the economic picture of that area, as are the Bedouins whose camps can be seen near Alexandria and who wander as traders in the Lybian desert. They perpetuate the traditions of their forebears, live in tents and periodically move within strictly circumscribed regions, their ancestral roaming grounds.

There are other groups, large families whose tribal antecedents are less obvious and not apparent at first glance. Their leading members often live highly sophisticated lives, travel and study abroad and tend to be at home in western as well as eastern society. The writer happened to mention the name of one of her Arab students in a conversation in Damascus; he was recognized immediately as a member of a "leading" and "influential" tribe. Begum Shah Nawaz, the fascinating woman leader and member of the Pakistani Legislative Assembly, proudly talked of the Arab origin of her "tribe," using this appellation repeatedly in its literal meaning. She stressed its importance for the effectiveness of her political work; as chairman of its "tribal council" (again her own expression) she represents one

million, four hundred thousand people, and her word accordingly carried considerable weight in public affairs.

The writer's hosts in the Egyptian village did not aim, as
a group, at influence in public affairs and politics, though one
of its members was at the time of her stay with them a member
of the Egyptian Senate. However, in their local communities
they were highly respected and regarded as leaders, elected, by
public acclaim, to communal offices, such as mayor (*'umdah*)
and head man of the district (*sheikh al-balad*). Even the less
desirable aspects of tribal customs were still apparent. In a
village, not far from her own and within the range of personal
observation, a protracted blood feud was raging (in 1950-51)
between two of its great families. During the whole period of
her stay, a large number of policemen had to be constantly on
duty to prevent further bloodshed, for each murder committed
in revenge provoked new retaliation. Once it seemed that a
conciliation, based on the time-honoured custom of blood-money,
had been achieved, but the hostilities flared up again. One of
the ancient "wars" in pre-Islamic Arabia was the exact counterpart of that modern blood feud, even in a small detail. One
man was not satisfied with the settlement of his claim in the
general peace treaty. He killed a member of the enemy's
family to settle his private account, with the same result as in
the modern Egyptian village.

To the scholar steeped in ancient Arabian lore, the warfare between the Israelis and the Arabs in the Gaza strip and
elsewhere, too, have a familiar ring. For raids, skirmishes and
small-scale fighting, treacherous murders and retaliation in revenge are the topics of the "Arab Battle Days" from which
the western scholars had derived their derogatory picture of
conditions in pre-Muhammadan Arabia.

III.

But that is not the whole picture. On the other hand, we
see the tribes gather peacefully at stated times at the annual
fairs to the greatest of which "all Arabia" flocked. There
were lesser ones, too, though they are, for that reason, less

frequently mentioned and all but forgotten; they had merely regional importance and attracted only certain tribes. Fairs were peaceful occasions; carrying arms was forbidden and enemies could feel reasonably safe from each other's attack. But many a time the fair was the scene of new provocation, the holy truce was not always kept. Treachery does not respect the sanctity of a truce nor the inviolability of the fair. Again the past and the present mingled in the writer's mind when she witnessed a man being stabbed to death in an ancient city far in the north of Pakistan. It happened in the midst of a gay crowd celebrating their country's Independence Day. Failure of electricity had suddenly plunged the whole city from brilliant illumination into almost complete darkness and the murderer was taking advantage of this opportunity to avenge a murder possibly committed years ago and not necessarily by the victim himself.

In their nomadic life, the Bedouins' very existence depended upon the camel which provided milk and meat for their sustenance and wool for weaving their tents and their clothes. It enabled them to wander in the desert when it was covered with vegetation after the spring, and less so, the autumn rains. In the villages of Egypt men and women still carry very primitive spindles made from a stick and a potsherd on which they spin camel's hair or sheep's wool while walking along a country road or chatting with each other. Pre-Islamic poetry reflects the importance of this animal for the Bedouin. The poet devoted one part of his ode to the praise of his mount that carried him on his raids and his peaceful travels through the desert, swift as an ostrich—and whoever has seen a unit of the camel corps in the desert will appreciate this comparison.

The Pre-Islamic Arab probably could not conceive of life without the camel, and even in the contemporary Near and Middle East in Egypt or in Syria, in the Punjab of Pakistan or in northern India, it is a familiar figure. Every evening, strings of these quaint, strangely fascinating animals used to come into Cairo from the *Rif*, twenty or thirty led by one or two fellaheen. They meandered through the fashionable suburbs into the centre of the city bearing their loads of products and vegetables, melons, cucumbers, dates, oranges, whatever was in season, to the city markets. However, the new order apparently has eliminated this attractive spectacle, at least from the main thoroughfares. Or, walking along a canal, one would meet them with one, or sometimes two and even more riders; then the ancient stories of the "Days of the Arabs" would come to mind when a man and his croup-rider would set out together for a raid. But, decidedly the ancient Bedouin never saw a sight like the famous camel carts in Karachi! He surely would have felt it to be an insult to his noble steed to subject it to the humiliating task of pulling a cart.

Nowadays this formerly indispensable animal is gradually being superseded by jeep and truck, bus, motor car, and aeroplane. In spite of its ubiquity in olden as well as modern times, the camel had not been the beast of burden and riding for the earliest nomads in history. Ass nomadism preceded camel nomadism, for pictorial representation of asses is found, as early as 1900 B.C., in murals at Beni Hasan in Upper Egypt, while our earliest inscriptional testimony to domesticated camels does not antedate the eleventh century B.C. The braying of the donkey still resounds in the cities and the countryside of the East everywhere. Carleton S. Coon stresses the epoch-making impact of the domestication of the camel for Arab civilization; he divides the history of the peninsula into three periods: "before camel, with camel and trade, and with camel and little trade."

At the peak period of its ancient civilization, trade in Arabia was only possible through this animal which carried its riches, ivory, spices and incense; its modern revival is taking place through the automobile and the aeroplane, in the service of the oil industry. But even in our age of sophisticated civilization, the camel has not wholly lost its importance for trade and communication. To this day, the caravans cross mountains and inaccessible lands where the car and the truck would find it difficult to pass. The caravan and the motor road

negotiate, side by side, the rugged, forbidding Khyber Pass;
the bazaar in Landikotal, the trading centre near the Afghan
border, encompasses a wide, sandy square where the caravan
driver can make his camel kneel to unload his wares, but
where the truck would find difficult going. Ancient Peshawar
City, as of old, has a caravan centre for the traders coming
down the pass.

IV.

It is obvious that such a distinctive social organization
developed its own social habits, customs, and codes of behaviour.
In such harsh surroundings, with life depending on hardiness,
courage, presence of mind and alertness, it is evident that these
qualities were admired and cultivated by both men and women.
Arab poetry and prose furnish abundant evidence for this.
The odes sing the praise of the valiant and wise leader, the
indomitable fighter for his own and his tribe's honour, the
hard-hitting, victorious hero; but they also extol self-sacrifice,
magnanimity, devotion and wisdom. Generosity, even to a
fault, was equally expected from any one who aspired to
greatness. The ancient term *mur'uwwah* "manliness," *virtus*,
expressed all that. Even Islam does not depict its hero *par
excellence* as meek. True, Muhammad is described as humble
(for he had been an orphan, as he himself stressed), in line
with pre-Islamic admiration for frugality; his concern for the
poor grew in the indigenous fertile ground of proverbial
generosity, and his opposition to amassing riches mirrors the
Arab's disdain of worldly possessions. But Muhammad was also
the leader in battle, the hard fighter of great personal courage.

The women, too, fitted into this life. They had to share
the hardships of nomadism and were burdened with the "domestic" tasks. They had to pitch the tents and strike camp,
they prepared the provisions for the raids and were charged
with the care for the water skins holding the indispensable
water supply. Frequently they were exposed to great personal
danger and underwent the humiliating experience of captivity.
But they could be certain that their close relatives and the
tribal community of which they formed part felt their captive

state as collective shame and dishonour. The prisoners of war knew that they would be redeemed even if it meant the sacrifice of all the tribe's possessions. Women, in that remote age, were an integral part of the communal life; segregation and seclusion, which impoverished and narrowed the life of Muslim women for centuries, were instituted much later.

V.

The necessities of commerce combined with opportunities afforded by nature to develop another stratum of social life in that desert land. In other, more favoured, regions of the Near East, cities and city states grew on the rivers flowing through them. Arabia has no perennial rivers; it knows only *wâdis,* river beds in which water flows intermittently at certain seasons or when the run-off of abundant rains in the mountains fills their dry course. Settlements could therefore only develop in an oasis where wells from underground water provided this indispensable commodity; there the caravans would rest their animals and replenish their water supply. From time immemorial, these oases had also been held to be the abode of the Divine, and had become sites of worship and of sanctuaries; these two factors combined to make them centres of social and religious life. The early resistance of the Meccans against Muhammad's religious appeal was caused by the fear lest their city lose its importance as a religious and trading centre. The Prophet's attack against their social customs and religious beliefs made this a very real danger.

These oases had attracted settlers. In the course of time, whole tribes had given up their nomadic existence and had become guardians of the sanctuary and traders. Various Near and Middle East governments are nowadays encouraging a similar process in order to cope with the problem of their Nomad population; they are thus consciously furthering, and possibly hastening, a continuous and almost instinctive process that had been going on from time immemorial as a natural, necessary phenomenon.

Since whole tribes would settle together, many, if not all,

features of their earlier organization would remain intact in their new environment. Closer communal life, in a much narrower area in which contacts were more intimate and un-avoidable, cried out for stricter organization; but only faint echoes are found in our sources, much of it legendary, at that. For obvious reasons, Mecca and Yathrib (the pre-Islamic name of Medînah) stand out in Muslim writings; from the earliest periods of Islam any reminiscence of the Prophet was cherished and therefore saved from oblivion. These two cities were glori-fied as the Prophet's own, and Khaibar and Tâ'if, too, shared in the fame for their lesser part in the drama. But there were in Arabia other, though smaller, localities with lesser fairs and sanctuaries not universally attended. It seems hardly credible that these should have been completely abandoned as soon as the festivities had ended and the visiting crowds departed, but our sources, even our oldest and most reliable authorities, would have us believe that. Again, definite judgement ought to be delayed until archaeology proves either the ancient writers, or those of us who do not give them their due credit, wrong.

These "cities" did not possess at that time an urban life comparable to that of medieval European towns. The four best-known settlements in Central Arabia, in the century in which Islam was born, were "cities" only in the sense that their inhabitants were settled and had occupations and interests that made their stay in them permanent. Neither Mecca nor Yathrib, for instance, was at that time surrounded by a wall. Indeed, in the third year after his Emigration to Medînah, Muhammad won the decisive victory over the Meccans in the so-called "Battle of the Ditch" (*Khandaq*) by a technique unknown in Arabian warfare. He defended the city with the help of a wall and a trench. Yathrib was an extended oasis with sprawling orchards and date groves that were famous and its main source of income; Khaibar was another such oasis to the north of Medînah, and Tâ'if served as a summer resort for the "fashion-able aristocracy" of Mecca. The latter seems to have had a fair-ly solid, coherent citizenry, a factor that counteracted Mu-hammad's revolutionary call considerably. However, it offered him, in its lower social strata, amongst the "clients" and the slaves, a fertile ground for his new gospel; with them he achieved his earliest success and from among them he gained his first followers.

VI.

While all descriptions of Mecca convey the picture of a "bourgeois" community with well-satisfied burghers, Yathrib offers that of a strife-torn, disrupted and utterly disorganized society. Its history is not only interesting in itself, and warrants attention as an example of oasis society, but has considerable bearing on modern concepts of state in Islam. For Muhammad's own ideas were shaped with Yathrib-Medînah in view; they became the foundation for later Islamic theories of state, and even philosophers took them as the model for their vision of the Ideal State.

Yathrib had originally been founded by Jewish tribes; three of these were still flourishing at the time of the Prophet's arrival. At a later period, nomads of South Arabian descent settled there and wrested supremacy from the Jews, though these retained both property and influence in the settlement. Eventually two factions dominated the oasis: the two leading Arab tribes, called respectively Aus and Khazraj, each with their dependent "sworn allies," and the three Jewish tribes with their dependents and allies. In the course of time, the Aus and the Khazraj became locked in protracted mortal feuds in which the Jews were also taking sides.

The very plan of the city contributed to this development. Each clan, some thirty or forty families, lived within their orchards and plantations, with wells for their own and their cattle's water supply. This arrangement alone would have furthered the rise of particular interests and impeded the growth of community spirit. Moreover, in time of danger, the clans would withdraw into specially prepared and fortified compounds provided with wells and stores of food and dominated by towerlike structures; there they could defend themselves, often for extended periods, against enemy attacks. Thus, the house of a Yathrib man was in a very real sense his castle.

In the accounts of his travels through South Arabia, the great contemporary explorer H. St. J. Philby describes similar conditions in the villages of Hadramawt; each house had become a fortress for defense against or attack on their neighbour, their enemy. To this day, the traveller through the Khyber Pass can see the half-hidden fortifications of the tribal "kings" and he is forewarned of the possibility of hostile reception (though the writer experienced only grace and friendliness, mingled with some good-natured curiosity, when her car in which she travelled with three other, Muslim, ladies stalled in the middle of a Pathan village, far up the Pass).

These feuds and warfares in Yathrib continued right into the Prophet's time. But the chaotic conditions carried in them, unbeknownst to the men and women suffering from them, the seed for future greatness. Without them, Yathrib would have remained forever an obscure oasis in a vast, impenetrable desert country. Through them, it was destined to bring fulfillment to the vision of one of mankind's great religious and political personalities.

CHAPTER TWO

The Religious Foundation

I.

The surviving literary sources contain only scarce evidence
of religious attitudes in pagan Arabia; hence, western scholarship has long assumed that the North Arabian in the centuries
preceding Islam had no deep religiosity. Yet, the Arab was not
the irreligious person unconcerned with good and evil or the
Divine and Transcendental, nor with his soul and his fate after
death, as which he is so frequently and erroneously described.
Because of Islamic censorship, Arab literature offers but scanty
references to religious beliefs; hardly any but the deities mentioned in the Koran and those worshipped in the Meccan
sanctuary, the Ka'bah, have escaped oblivion.

Yet, what little knowledge did survive shows that pre-Islamic Arabian religious expression conforms to ancient Near
Eastern tradition. Evidence for this is preserved in the Koran
itself, though only five gods, Wadd, Su'âh, Yaghûth, Ya'ûq,
and Nasr (Sûrah 71, verse 23) and three goddesses, Allât,
Manât, and al-'Uzzà (Sûrah 53, verse 23), are mentioned in the
holy Book. Unconsciously, Muhammad reveals old beliefs, not
only in his attacks against these idols. Traditional formulas
live on, especially in the very early times, when he swears
"By the snorting chargers" or "By the heaven and its towers";
ancient mythological concepts compel him to call upon "the
sun, the moon and the stars," the ancient Semitic triad of
gods, as his witnesses. Even the heavenly "ship" is still alive
in his mind (Sûrah 14, verse 36; Sûrah 36, verse 40f.).

Passionately he condemns the custom of burying new-born

47

daughters (Sûrah 81, verse 8f.; S.16, 61) "for fear of penury"
(S.17, v. 33). Female infanticide is also attested to elsewhere in
Arabic literature; it is the Arabian version of fertility rites
known, in one form or another, from all parts of the world
including the ancient Near East. The Koranic attribution to
fear of penury has been misunderstood by both Muslims and
non-Muslims. The Arab was thought to have buried his infant
daughter for economic reasons. Muslim interpretation further
explained the custom by the Arab's fear of disgrace if she were
captured and exposed to the humiliations of captivity. However, neither inability to provide for her, nor dislike of daughters
as such, nor even the fear of disgrace, were the motives for this
act, the former notions as far from the Arab's mind then as
now. By burying his new-born daughter, he wished to impart
the life-giving, productive power inherent in the female to the
earth.

Muhammad detested this heathen rite because he had reached
a higher stage of religiosity beyond the need for magic and
superstition. Creation, Life and Death, all productivity on
earth, were to him evidence of the Divine Power, of Allâh's
ability to perform these miracles. Burial of female infants
cannot have been an ancient rite, forgotten or half-forgotten in
the Prophet's time, as both early Islamic and modern apologists
would have us believe; had that been so, the Prophet would
not have felt compelled to inveigh against it so passionately
(Sûrah 81, verse 8f.) nor so frequently (Sûrah 6, 137ff; 6, 141;
6, 152; 17, 33, 43, 16). It must have been practiced in his time
and he must have witnessed it as a living custom.

Nor is the Koranic prohibition of the *maisir* game and of
fermented beverages (*khamr*) an abhorrence of the sin of gam-
bling and drinking, or the prohibition of partaking of pork a
sanitary precaution, as is so often asserted. Granted, Muhammad's social conscience was wide awake; but for that he found
other outlets: the orphan, the widow and the divorcee, the
poor and the blind were the objects of his social care. The
vine and the pig were accessories in idolatrous cults and the
maisir game with its casting of arrows and its slaughter of camels

was a survival, in attenuated form, of sacrifices and rituals combined with divination; hence they belonged to the condemned idol worship.

II.

More than anything else do the ceremonies in Mecca and its sanctuary, the Ka'bah, the holiest of holy in Islam, preserve the memory of pre-Islamic paganism, with its rites intact. Judaism and Christianity, too, commemorate ancient rites, sacrifices or processions; in all three faiths, the contents of their ritual was sublimated and re-interpreted to such an extent that the worshipper is no longer conscious of their original significance and the scholar has to seek deep to reconstruct their ancient meanings. How many in the Jewish congregation will remember the two sacred stones carried in the Ark of the Covenant when the scrolls of the Torah are lifted up for all to see on a Sabbath morning? The worshippers of today are aware solely of the ethical and moral message of the Law, not of the fetish of ancient Israel. The Meccan rites, too, have long ago found a new interpretation.

The rites and ceremonies of the pilgrimage to Mecca, the *Hajj*, are, in our own days, the same as they were in Muhammad's life time and a millennium before even the Prophet performed them. The circumambulation of the Ka'bah, the *tawâf*, is symbolic of the solemn affirmation by the worshipper of the deity's sovereignty and of his readiness for its service. It is a declaration of mutual dedication: man affirms his devotion to the deity and is, by this act, assured of its protection and its life-giving power. The worshipper kissing the Black Stone in the Ka'bah, touching it with his hand or pressing his body to the holy House, feels the inherent power and immanent "blessing" *barakah* penetrate his body and soul. For the same reason, the modern Egyptian fellaheen will press around Naguîb or 'Abd Nâsir ("Nasser"), the devout Hindu will touch the holy man, the pious Jew press his prayer shawl to the Torah scroll and then put it to his lips, or the Roman Catholic kiss the bishop's ring. The custom of the Egyptian student to kiss the hand of his teacher or of the younger scholar to bend over that of the older, venerated master is an attenuated form of the same feeling.

Amazingly, in spite of strong liberal tendencies and intense discussion of modern ideas and progressive thought, contemporary Muslims have never questioned the validity of the Ka'bah or the justification of the ceremonies of the pilgrimage within Islamic monotheism. The re-interpretation in Islamic terms of its rituals and the places where they are performed or their connexion with the patriarch Abraham were not introduced by modern apologists, but originated with the Prophet himself. No contemporary Muslim writer has published a critical evaluation of the *Hajj* and its central position in Muslim religiosity. Taha Husain (1889-   ), the leading Egyptian liberal whom one might expect to do so, does not touch on this vital point; nor does the moderate modernist Muhammad Husain Heikal (1888-1956) discuss this problem in his *Life of Muhammad*. Yet, this biography was expressly written in answer to the demand of Muslim youth of the twentieth century for a new interpretation of the Prophet's personality and his creed, one that they could accept and align with their modern rationalism. Muhammad Iqbâl (died 1938), the most influential religious thinker of our times in Muslim India, a founder of Pakistan, whose philosophy and literary work inspired liberal thought, does not devote a sentence of his *Lectures on the Reconstruction of Religious Thought in Islam* to this central rite which unites the Muslim world as nothing else does in Islam. In his philosophic poem *The Secret of the Self* and in others of his poetic works, the Ka'bah is used as a symbol but not viewed in its actuality.

Does that imply that Mecca and the pilgrimage have lost their meaning for contemporary Islam or at least for the educated modern Muslim? Any one who has lived in a Muslim country of whatever shade of orthodoxy will emphatically deny this inference. Modern pilgrims to Mecca have written about their experience in moving terms, through which the ecstasy they felt in the hallowed places during the sacred ceremonies is imparted to the sensitive reader, though he may not be a Believer. Western-educated scholars will relate their emotion to the sense of historical continuity symbolized by the Ka'bah. All around him in Muslim lands, the visitor will find proofs of the depth of the emotion; the excited anticipation of departing pilgrims, the light that shone in the eyes of an educated woman pilgrim when she remembered her pilgrimage to Mecca, or the psychosomatic nervous symptoms of a simpler woman pilgrim amongst the writer's friends, were evidence of the deep spiritual emotion it had evoked.

Throughout the Muslim world, the Great Festival of Sacrifices, the culmination of the pilgrimage season, is celebrated with piety, devotion and gaiety. For weeks, countless thousands of sheep and goats have been driven into the cities to be fattened for the sacrifice, on that day, in mosques and private houses, at the hour when Meccan pilgrims are offering their sacrifices in Minà. They are gaily daubed with brilliant blue, vermillion and yellow dye just as in antiquity the sacrificial animals were decorated with colorful ribbons, as the poets tell us. That morning, the mosques throughout the world are filled to overflowing; even in Istanbul, the guide boasted that the huge court of the Sulaimâniyah Mosque was insufficient to hold the crowds of worshippers. The service in Lahore's Shahi Mosque, which allegedly has the largest court of any mosque in the world, is attended by tens of thousands, and everywhere the smaller mosques are filled to capacity.

But even more moving was the simple sunrise service held in the open desert by the village people of the writer's Egyptian home. Long before sunrise, high folk and low assembled in quiet dignity on the wide ground at the foot of a hill—just as the pilgrims in Mecca were "standing" ceremoniously at the foot of the Mountain of Mercy at 'Arafât, or as the Israelites had been "standing" at the foot of Mount Sinai. The villagers were imitating the scene at 'Arafât as closely as possible, performing the prayers prescribed for this festival. They were listening to their *sheikh* preaching a sermon on its significance as a commemoration of Abraham's willingness to sacrifice his

son Ishmael (as the Muslims believe). He reminded the congregation that Allâh in His mercy accepted the ram as a substitute for the human sacrifice. After the service, the householders
slaughtered their sheep or goat and distributed some of the
meat amongst the poor. The day was then spent cheerfully,
visiting and receiving friends and relatives; a wedding and a
circumcision ceremony were held in the village during the days
of the festival.

Modern Muslims emphasize Mecca's decisive role as the
centre of the Muslim world, the focus for the whole community
of Islam; as of old, the deep longing of every Believer is to
fulfill, once in his life, the obligation of performing the *Hajj*,
one of the "pillars" of his faith. Each year, to this day, at the
beginning of the pilgrimage season, an impressive ceremony
takes place in Cairo. The caravan carrying the Cover of the
Ka'bah, of black cloth with Koran verses embroidered in gold,
is sent on its way with military pomp and honours, in the
presence of religious and secular dignitaries. The whole village
turns out to accompany the departing pilgrims, with banners
and bands of musicians, for part of their way, if only to the
railway station; on their return, they are greeted with equally
joyful celebration. They will decorate their houses with vivid,
though often rather primitive, paintings commemorating their
experience. The pilgrim has become a person of standing in
his village henceforth to be addressed respectfully with the
title of *Hâjjî*.

Thus, Muslims consider performing the pilgrimage their
sacred duty and the crowning experience of their religious life;
highly educated, cultured and sophisticated men and women
have described the rites and ceremonies at the House of Allâh
in Mecca as the culmination of their spiritual experience.
Though the writer, being Jewish, cannot go to Mecca, she has
witnessed, in Delhi, a ceremony of comparable religious emotion, though differing in its ceremonial as well as its ancient
roots. It was the commemoration, by Shî'î Muslims, of the
martyrdom of the Prophet's grandson Husain who was treacher-
ously murdered at Kerbelâ' together with many members of

'Alî's family. Her hosts, a group of Shî'ites of high rank, seemed to be as deeply affected by the stirring ceremonies, the chanting and beating of breasts, the recital of the martyrologies, in prose and poetry, as the rest of the crowd filling the Shî'î shrine. It must be confessed, however, that even the Jewish spectator was gripped by the exciting ritual and had a hard time to keep her hands from beating her breast to the hypnotizing rhythm of the dirges.

III.

Though Islam thus rose from the native soil, giving new meaning and new direction to ancient beliefs, it was not a mere re-interpretation of Arab paganism. By proclaiming the Unity of Allâh, Muhammad introduced a basically new principle; for though the ancient Arab recognized and worshipped Him, He was, for them, only one of many gods. For Muhammad, He was not merely *primus inter pares,* worshipped, among other, less generally acknowledged, deities by most Arab tribes and in most parts of Arabia. He was the one and only God, the Lord of the Universe Who has no equal nor associate. This call to monotheism resounds like a clarion throughout the Koran.

This God was the All-Powerful, He Who created man from a blood clot, the miracle that proves His power of creation as well as of re-creation. The wonder of birth is at the same time the explanation and proof for the greater, though hitherto un-experienced, miracle of re-birth, of resurrection after death. In this insistence in the sequence of Birth—Death—Resurrection, Muhammad was a true child of the Near East. No need to claim Jewish origin for the emphasis on this idea in Islam; from the most remote Egyptian antiquity, this myth of death and resurrection permeates all Near Eastern mythology. To the Meccans, sceptical of the possibility of physical resurrection, Muhammad shows proof for Allâh's power to do this: the won-drous yearly revival of the earth, after the heat of the sun and the thirst of summer had killed its vitality, is evidence of His power to perform the greater miracle of resurrection after death. To Muhammad, this "sign" is conclusive proof of Allâh's omnipotence allowing no contradiction.

The Koran, the holy Scripture of Islam, reflects Muhammad's development from religious meditation to passionate visionary and warner; it mirrors the propagator and defender of the Faith who became the organizer of a religious community and the founder of a political state organization. The early history of the Prophet's life is shrouded in darkness and thinly veiled legend whence factual historical truth can hardly be guessed at; the history of his inner life and of his spiritual growth since Allâh had called him to be His Messenger to the Meccans is distinctly outlined in the Koran.

The Muslims themselves recognize two major phases in Muhammad's development. His call on his Meccan contemporaries to worship Allâh and his struggle for recognition in his native town mark the first epoch. Then followed ten years passed in Yathrib, the Prophet's City, after his emigration from Mecca in 622 A.D. to the time of his death in 632. Each chapter of the Koran, called a *Sûrah,* carries at its head a statement whether it was "revealed" in Mecca or in Medînah. Modern western scholarship recognizes more specific indications in the Koran that make it possible to distinguish various phases in the Prophet's religious development.

His earliest sermons reflect the passion of his inner vision when he first received Allâh's awe-inspiring call. They mirror his fear of the approaching Hour of Judgement, the Day when all creation will be called before His throne and when all mankind will have to answer for their deeds. Good will then find its reward, evil will be punished. On that Day, the tombs will discard their dead, the moon will be split and the stars tumble down from the firmament. In beautiful, poetic, passionate and vigorous language does Muhammad pour out his visions in this first period.

The Prophet was deeply convinced that Allâh had sent him to his people to warn them of the impending doom and exhort them to repent so that the calamity might be averted. The Sûrahs of the second period reflect this struggle with the Meccans. Instead of believing him and heeding his warning, the Meccans derided Muhammad's assertion that the dead could be resurrected and that the unbelievers would be punished by hellfire. In despair and anxiety, Muhammad recounted the fate meted out to former generations and ancient peoples. Like his contemporaries, they had disregarded the warnings of Allâh's messengers and had persisted in their evil ways; they had perished and their cities had been destroyed. These "legends of divine punishment" are reiterated in the Koran and are characteristic for the second period of the Prophet's activity; they continue to be a theme of his sermons in the third period. Even after the *Hijrah,* the Prophet's emigration to Medînah, the Koran returns to this theme, but mainly in brief allusions, almost like a refrain, as a reminder of a well-known theme.

The period before his departure from Mecca, in western terminology the third, is characterized by arguments and polemics against the Meccans. In this epoch, a certain despair and discouragement can be sensed in the revelations, and Muhammad needs Allâh's assurance that he cannot be held responsible for his lack of success: "What! canst thou make the deaf to hear, or guide the blind, or him who is in obvious error?" (Sûrah 43, verse 39). "For Allâh guides aright whom He chooses and leads astray whom He chooses." Thus, His Messenger is powerless.

IV.

With the change in environment and the new tasks that awaited the Prophet in Medînah, the whole character of his message changed. Called to Yathrib not so much in answer to his religious appeal, but on account of its social and political potentialities, Muhammad developed from the religious ecstatic and visionary into the far-sighted political leader. In spite of the difficulties he had encountered in his native town, the great universal appeal of his idea had become evident. No longer should tribe or social class divide the Arabs; Islam would abolish pagan particularism. By accepting Islam, every Muslim would become the equal and brother of every other

Believer, regardless of his origin or social standing. This was an entirely new concept in the Arab social structure where any allegiance beyond the narrow confines of the tribe and its associates was unknown.

For Muhammad, the concept of brotherhood in Islam was not a goal to be reached in some ideal future; he tried to achieve it in his own circle by practical means. Already in Mecca, he had instituted "brotherhood" between Muslims not bound to each other by bonds of blood; in a solemn ceremony, thus we are told in ancient sources, he proclaimed pairs of followers as brethren, and imposed stringent obligations of mutual support and help outside and beyond the demands of tribe and family. In Medînah, "brotherhood" was used to weld "Immigrants" and native citizens together. This concept of Brotherhood in Islam was expressed in the ringing words "Every Muslim is a brother to every other Muslim" in the oldest authentic document preserved besides the Koran, the so-called "Charter of Medînah," of which Muhammad is the author. It is still the strongest link between the diverse components that make up the modern Muslim community.

From its inception, Islam contained that element of universality that is still characteristic for it. It aimed at the unification of mankind, though this term embraced only that part of humanity known to Muhammad. Already in Mecca, this principle had met with a measure of success; indeed, it was one of the reasons for the hostility of the Quraish, the Prophet's own tribe, and, according to legend, the aristocrats of the city. Tribes outside Mecca had sworn allegiance to him; their defection after his death showed that they had not been attracted by the prophetic message of the new religion but, in the ancient Arabian tradition, by Muhammad's reputation as a leader. The inhabitants of faction-ridden Yathrib called this man of proven ability to their city to act as a peace maker.

In his new environment, the Prophet had to deal with social and political questions, with problems of law and justice, with immediate decisions in cases of litigation. His task was to weld the three elements constituting the citizenry into one community; these were the Aus and the Khazraj, who had called him and who were henceforth called "Helpers" in honour of that merit, the Jews and the "Immigrants" from Mecca. In the Charter of Medînah, he gave his *Ummat al-Islâm* "Community of Islam" a workable constitution which is remarkable for its wise restraint as well as its sound approach to the problem. Only after having established Islam, with himself as its undisputed head, did he consolidate this group and his hold on it by eliminating the Jewish element in the city through the only cruel and deplorable, though necessary, act in his whole career.

This remarkable document deserves a more detailed discussion. Its text is preserved in full only in the earliest extant biography of the Prophet by Muhammad ibn Ishâq (died 768 A.D.) though there are excerpts from, and references to, it in two or three other works. The original document does not seem to have been preserved (though one may be forgiven for hoping that that precious relic may yet be unearthed in some archive buried in the dry sands of Arabia or hidden in a cave), but the authenticity of the text as copied in the Prophet's *Biography* is assured for internal reasons. The most convincing argument for its genuineness is the moderation in style as well as in the demands made on the contracting parties. Through this charter, Muhammad assumes leadership in a strictly circumscribed and limited field, in the relations between the inhabitants of Yathrib; he is merely the arbitrator between the parties to whom conflicts affecting communal life were to be submitted. The guarantor for this constitution is Allâh, the only religious phrase found in the document, expressed in somewhat archaic Arabic; the parties to the treaty submit to its terms as Believers and Muslims.

The Jews were incorporated into the community of Islam as equals; they had the same claim to protection by the other participants in the charter and identical obligations towards them. Their sub-groups and clans were listed in as careful detail as were those of the Arabs. Most important, they were explicitly guaranteed the right to remain Jews, probably the world's first documented granting of religious liberty.

The document was addressed to the Believers in Yathrib as opposed to the "rest of mankind" *min dûna-n-nâs,* that is, any group outside those enumerated in the charter and, in particular, the Meccans. It exempted the signatories from submitting to Muhammad for arbitration any conflict between them and an outside foe, as long as the Muslim community as such was not affected or involved. All these factors are evidence for the authenticity of this document as well as its early date: it was drafted during the first year of Muhammad's residence in Yathrib. A later forger could not have conceived of any limitation to the Prophet's power; he would have been anxious to show him as the dominant figure in the "Prophet's City," as Yathrib later was called exclusively. But the charter used the ancient appellation throughout. No forger would have admitted that the Jews had had equal status in the community, after the Koran had branded them as obstructors of the Prophet's mission and after they had been eliminated from the city. The charter of Medînah thus is one of the most valuable historical instruments for reconstructing the earliest history of Islam.

It is even more important yet. It is a landmark in the development of Islam as a political concept which actually begins with it and which again has assumed such importance in our own time. In particular, it holds several elements of interests for the modern community of Islam. It contains the germ for the separation of national concerns from those of the religious *Ummah* which in principle should be, though not in fact are, common to all Muslim nations. It also shows an early comprehension of the necessity for social and political integration of minority groups into the body politic without depriving them of their religious freedom. It is remarkable that an Arab in the seventh century A.D. should have understood that. The Prophet's outstanding ability as a political leader emerges from the charter as it does from the Koran; the former expressed it in legal terms, while the latter, even in the Medinian period, still remains inspirational.

In consequence of his break with the Jews after his victory over the Meccans in the "Battle of the Ditch" (Khandaq), Muhammad began to emphasize his Arab heritage. Turning to the cult at Mecca and its centre, the Ka'bah, he changed the direction of prayer from that towards Jerusalem, formerly adopted to attract the Jews, to that towards the Meccan sanctuary. He further exchanged the 'Âshûrâ' fast day, with Jewish overtones, for Ramadhân, the month of fasting, possibly with ancient Arabian religious associations. These Arab factors in Islam, to this day, dominate Islamic cult. For the first time in their history the Arabs gained a feeling of Arab unity and national direction.

From this period also dated the emphasis put on Abraham (Ibrâhîm), the pre-revelation believer in the Oneness of God, as the builder of the Ka'bah and the founder of its cult. Through this connexion with the Biblical patriarch, it was rendered compatible with the strict monotheism of Islam, in spite of its latent paganism. In this effort Muhammad succeeded completely. The modern Muslim is no longer conscious of its pagan contents; for him, the stations of the Meccan ceremonies are intimately related to Abraham, the venerated "Friend of Allâh," and his son Ishmael.

V.

For the later religious and political development of Islam, its concept of the Prophet's personality and the prophetic office is of special importance. Muslims rightly resent hearing their faith called "Mohammedanism" or themselves described as "Mohammedans"; these terms seem to make the Prophet himself an object of veneration and of worship. Nothing can be farther from the true spirit of Islam or more opposed to the intentions of its founder. For Muhammad never transgressed the boundaries set for ordinary mortals. He refused to be provoked into claiming the ability to perform miracles. Nor did he assert to possess the gift of prophecy, though he called himself a *nabî*, and later, the *Nabî*; following the customary translation of this word, Muhammad has been accorded the title of The Prophet.

But this term has a somewhat different connotation in western usage derived from Rabbinic, Judaeo-Christian tradition, from what it conveyed to the ancient Semite. The true ancient meaning of this term is "One who is called (by God), one who has a vocation from God." According to William F. Albright, "This interpretation of the word suits its meaning exactly; the prophet was the man who felt himself called by God for a special mission in which his will was subordinated to the will of God which was communicated to him by direct inspiration." This comment perfectly describes the self-appraisal of Allâh's Messenger and the mental image of him that orthodox Islamic theology preserved throughout the centuries.

This, however, is not the whole picture. Though the medieval theologians were primarily concerned with metaphysical quests, such as that for the essence of Allâh, the figure of the Prophet himself did not remain unchanged and unaffected. In the course of time, popular yearning for the transcendental adorned his image, even in orthodox, Sunnî, Islam, with many legendary traits; though faculties transgressing his limitations as a *human* being were shunned, extraordinary power and ability, sinlessness and the working of miracles were attributed to him. But he was never exalted into a deity, the son of God or a participant in God's glory, though both Near Eastern heritage and Gnostic and Hellenistic influence might have caused such deification. Sunnism, that is the main branch of Islam that had developed directly from Muhammad's own teaching through "following the Prophet's example," never contemplated him outside his human contexts; he remained thus forever man, albeit perfect and the perfect model.

Not so in Shî'ism. More than perfection and sinlessness was needed to satisfy the deep religious yearning of the Muslim masses. The Prophet's own attitude, expressed as Word of Allâh in the Koran, manifestly forbade endowing him with qualities unattainable by mortals, even though divinely inspired; the Faithful therefore had to search for some other person close to the Prophet to whom they might attribute them. 'Alî, the Prophet's cousin and son-in-law, satisfied this need. In the course of development, popular belief eventually placed 'Alî outside the human range and endowed him with all but divinity.

The Shî'î movement has political and religious facets. Politically, the *Shî'at 'Alî,* that is " 'Alî's Party," is due to Muhammad's neglect to designate a successor to his leadership. This omission calls for reflection on the concept Muhammad had of his office. At the time of his death, he was in his sixties, by the standards of his time and surroundings a very old man; moreover, he had been ailing for some time. It is almost inconceivable that he should not have contemplated death, especially as he had never regarded himself as exempt from human fate. Tradition preserved the sermon the Prophet is said to have preached in Mecca at the Pilgrimage of Leavetaking, the last he undertook. In it he allegedly pronounced some fundamental principles of Islam; but tradition does not record any reference to the question of his succession.

Muhammad's evident statesmanship throughout his career should have manifested to him the importance of appointing a successor for the continuity of the community. However, in this respect, as in so many others, Muhammad proved to be a real Arab for whom leadership rested in the personality of the chief, not in the office as such. To him, as in ancient Arabia, leadership was based on voluntary recognition of outstanding, proven ability not attainable by any inherent right or privilege nor to be gained through inheritance or by virtue of blood kinship. The most decisive factor, however, was certainly Muhammad's conviction of having been chosen, "called" by Allâh; he may have trusted that his successor would equally be chosen by Him. For this reason, one of many, Shî'î assertions in direct statements or obliquely, through anecdotes, that the Prophet himself had willed 'Alî's succession, are evidently not based on historical fact; they lack both historical and inner truth.

But the Prophet forgot that he himself had been instrumental in changing the mentality of his followers. Out of members of many tribes, he had created one community. Yet, by his lack of foresight he furthered the re-emergence of rivalries still alive among the various factions that only his personality had been able to suppress. Within the hour of his death the wrangle for his succession began. Only 'Umar's quick grasp of the dangerous situation saved the community from disintegrating then and there. As our sources describe the scene, he took Abû Bekr's hand and paid homage to him, thus saving the day. The other contestants followed suit and through them the groups whose interests they represented. 'Umar's forceful personality also secured the succession for himself after Abû Bekr's death. When he felt that his own time had come, he wisely appointed an "Electoral College" to choose his successor from among them, a procedure entirely new for Arabia. By that time, however, the conviction that 'Alî should have been "by right" the Prophet's successor had crystallized into an organized movement that kept the struggle for the political ascendency of the 'Alid family going, in actual fight, for a long time, ideologically, forever.

Gradually, the Shî'î movement claimed even more. To it, 'Alî was the rightful heir to the Prophet's mantle, not only for sharing his blood, but for participating in the divine spark that had kindled the divine light in Muhammad and had made him the recipient of Allâh's Revelation.

This religious idea of Shî'ism has remained a powerful emotion in our own day. Its political ambitions were destroyed for all times, the emergence of Shî'ite dynasties and the existence of Shî'ite nations to this day notwithstanding, in the massacre at Kerbelâ'. For Shî'ism gained whatever political reality it possessed, in the past or at present, only long after the Islamic empire had passed its zenith; it never held sway over the whole expanse of Islam, as the Sunnah did and does. The Fâtimides in North Africa and Egypt, the Safawides and their successors in Iran, the Zaidî Imâms in Yemen in our own age, held and are holding only small parts of the vast former empire.

Shî'î spiritual power, however, emerged victorious from the tragedy at Kerbelâ'; indeed, it derived from it. It rests on two ideas, both indigenous to the East from remotest antiquity, and therefore able to penetrate into this form of Islam. They are the identity of the king and the god, and the idea of the god's death and resurrection. These beliefs are apparent in all ancient Near Eastern religions and those derived from them, though sometimes modified or attenuated, yet still clearly recognizable.

For the Shî'ah, 'Alî became the participant in the Divine, the receptacle of the divine spark that from of yore was believed to be immanent in kingship. Muhammad left no son to whom to bequeath this "divine light"; through his cousin 'Alî and his wife, the Prophet's daughter Fâtimah, his grandsons Hasan and Husain, the martyr of Kerbelâ', inherited it. From Husain, the divine light passed into the Imâm, a member of the 'Alide family in each of the following generations; according to Shî'î belief, either the seventh or the twelfth Imâm, who disappeared and remains hidden, will reappear at the end of days. Then, the Hidden Imâm, as the Mahdî, will, like the Jewish Messiah or Christ at His Second Coming, restore righteousness in the world and lead it to peace and justice.

The Mahdî idea (which is also alive in Sunnî Islam, but without its 'Alide connotations) was used throughout the centuries as a rallying point for various socio-religious and political movements. Social reformers or revolutionaries proclaimed themselves as the Mahdî promised to appear to lead the Muslims against the forces of evil. From ancient to modern times pretenders fought against the ruling religious as well as political powers, and against social injustice and evil. The best-known example in modern times is the Mahdî movement in the Sûdân where a descendant of the self-styled Mahdî plays again an important role.

Shî'î religion took, and still takes, its greatest inspiration from the martyrdom of Husain at Kerbelâ'. Historically, the massacre was the result of an ill-advised, premature, and therefore unsuccessful attempt to capture the caliphate for the 'Alide faction. Husain with some seventy other members of 'Alî's family and an insufficient number of adherents left Medînah for a campaign against the Umaiyad caliph Yazîd ibn Mu'âwiyah. At Kerbelâ', near the Euphrates, sixty miles southwest of Baghdad, he encamped to wait for the promised reinforcement. But before it reached him, Yazîd's forces attacked the camp and killed every man, woman and child. This tragic event lent itself pre-eminently to dramatic representation that became the centre of the commemorative celebrations of the Shî'î Passion Week. The first ten days of the month of Muharram, sacred days already in ancient Arabia, are dedicated to the "mourning for Husain" and the martyrs of Kerbelâ'. Merged into it are elements of great antiquity in Near Eastern religious myth. The Shî'î ceremonies evoke echoes of the death and resurrection idea of the Osiris myth as of the mourning for Adonis. In Shî'ism, the resurrection is projected into the eschatological time of the Return of the Mahdî.

In 1955, the writer spent the first eight days of that period in Lahore, Punjab, and the culminating day, the tenth of Muharram, traditionally considered the day of Husain's martyrdom, in Delhi. Since modern western witnesses and descriptions of the ceremonies seem to be rare, and modern Shî'îs whom one meets in the West usually deny that they are still celebrated in the traditional manner, the following excerpts from her diary may not be devoid of interest:

"During the first days of the month, large tents of black awning were erected in the gardens of several private houses. Each night, people gather there to mourn for Husain and listen to the recitation of poems and martyrologies. In the evening of the seventh Muharram, I drove with Mr. S. to the Walled City to watch the ceremonies in commemoration of Hazrat Husain's departure for battle. We left the car outside the gate and walked through narrow, crowded lanes lined with the shops of bakers, spice vendors and tailors to an *Imâmbârâ* or House of the Imâm. Though at first I thought I was entering a mosque, it was a private house decorated with the special features of the occasion and thereby transformed into a sanctuary. On three sides of the rectangular court were rooms in which the women were assembled, hidden behind bamboo screens. On the fourth side several men were sitting on a platform smoking hookahs and probably gossiping. The whole place was brightly lit by red and green electric lights and decorated

with green and black banners (the Shî'î colours), green plants
and red flowers. The banners were embroidered with Persian
inscriptions extolling the Ahl-i-Bait (Muhammad's and 'Alî's
family); a large outstretched "Hand of Fâtimah" topped the
largest of these. On one side, I saw a representation of the camp
and battlefield at Kerbelâ', typical for this festival, looking
somewhat like a Christmas crêche. There were no figures or
representations of any kind, but a few plants and flowers were
arranged in its background and candles were burning inside
its front part. The whole arrangement was brightly illumi-
nated by electricity and decorated with bunting and banners.
When I asked what the candles meant, my friends only answered: "We put candles there to express our reverence for
Hazrat Husain," but could give no other explanation. They
reminded me somewhat of the candles lit by Jews and Roman
Catholics for the souls of their dead.

"In the streets, crowds were milling around, and the *Imâmbârâ* was also full of people, amongst others, hawkers selling
garlands of flowers with which to decorate Husain's horses.
My friends gave me some for that purpose. After a while, I went
up to the roof to watch the procession from there together with
some thirty or more other women and children. It consisted
of several men carrying banners and others leading two white,
garlanded and caparisoned, saddled but riderless horses. (On
the tenth of Muharram, Husain's horse returned from the
battlefield saddleless, riderless.) The crowd pressed around them
and followed them touching banner and horses to derive *barakah* "blessing" from them; they were led into every *Imâmbârâ*
and into the courts of many other houses. After they had
passed, the streets remained quiet until the procession came
round again, for they make the circuit of the city seven times.
The man leading the horses and the people were chanting
dirges; whenever the names of 'Alî, Hasan or Husain were heard,
people would beat their breasts with both hands. Nonetheless,
on the whole, the atmosphere was not one of mourning but
rather of somewhat subdued gaiety. . .

"Colonel Z. called for me on the tenth to take me to the

Muharram ceremonies, the first to take place in Delhi since Partition. We drove into the old part of Delhi near the Great Mosque where the procession of the *Ta'zîyah* began. At first, I had thought that my companions were attending the ceremonies as a favour for me, but I soon realized that they were very serious about it. A number of young men, naked to the waist, had formed a circle round a large, light-green banner, called the *ta'zîyah,* carried by some others; it was garlanded and its middle pole ended in a *tughrah,* the stylized writing of the names of the 'Alides, topped by the word *Allâh.* People from the large crowd accompanying the *ta'zîyah* were touching it again and again; then they wiped their faces and those of their children with their hand to impart the *barakah* gained from it to their children.

"The young men were chanting dirges and invocations and were beating their bare breasts rhythmically with their hands; already they were bleeding, some only a little, but others already quite considerably. Every once in a while, at stated intervals, the procession would stop; then the youths whipped themselves with long leather thongs that had heavy metal ends, flinging them high over their heads to the rhythm of their chants. The blows landed on their bare backs with no nonsense about its being only pretense. By and by their backs and cheeks and breasts were bleeding profusely and one saw the deep weals and cuts. The chanting and the flagellation was directed by a leader who later in the *Imâmbârâ* recited a poetic eulogy on Husain of his own and became so excited that he had to be quieted by a member of the official party with whom I was attending the ceremonies. Slowly the procession moved on, taking nearly three hours for a distance that ordinarily could be covered in less than fifteen minutes.

"All along the passion road, the chanting and beating and flagellation continued without interruption. It passed through a quarter formerly inhabited by Muslims, but now occupied by Sikhs whose permission the police had procured before allowing the ceremonies to be held there. They were lining the streets and watching quietly and reverently. This is particu-

larly significant since at the time of Partition the hostility
between Sikhs and Muslims was merciless.

"In the *Imâmbârâ*, I sat down on the floor of the platform
with the men, the only woman there and decidedly the only
Jewish person present. The other women were gathered sepa-
rately on the roof, in accordance with the Muslim practice of
segregation of women. Hidden behind carpets was the replica
of Kerbelâ' to which the *ta'zîyah* was to be brought. When
it arrived, a great moaning and sobbing and weeping rose
from the congregation. The flagellants carried it into the
centre of the *Imâmbârâ* where they were beating their breasts
and swinging the thongs to the rhythm of their chanting and
the calling out of the martyrs' names in a climactic frenzy. Then,
quite suddenly, they stopped and the *ta'zîyah* was carried
around the sanctuary to be seen and touched by every one
present. With this, the official ceremony was ended. But the
assembly stayed on listening to the recital of poetry by a well-
known poet who enacted the story and emphasized its high
points with dramatic gestures. That must have been the way
in which poetry was recited in ancient days at the fairs of the
Arabs, and I suddenly understood why the poets were able to
rouse the emotions of the Arab crowds assembled there."

VI.

The almost indissoluble entwinement of religious ideas
and political emotions, one of the most fascinating features of
ancient Islam, found its counterpart in modern Islamic movements. It was apparent in Sunnî as well as in Shî'î Islam; in
medieval times, religious and dogmatic differences repeatedly
led to riots, revolutions, dethronement of rulers. Caliphs did
not shun to enforce religious beliefs by punishing, imprisoning
and torturing venerated religious leaders, philosophers or theologians who would not conform with their edicts regulating religious beliefs. In the contemporary states of Muslim persuasion,
theological disagreement may still be used to foster revolutions
or to force disliked governments out of power; religious bans
may be aimed at intimidating political adversaries. The Azhar

sheikhs in Cairo who threaten to excommunicate any Muslim who would make peace with Israel, or the various Muslim groups in Indonesia that are fighting for political power with religious slogans, are directing their religious zeal towards secular aims. But they are not "using" religion; they are convinced that their way is the only one that can justly claim to represent true Islam.

In recent years a striking example of this fact was given in Pakistan. In 1953, rioting broke out in Lahore and other towns of the Punjab resulting in bloodshed, with a number of persons killed and many more wounded. Martial law had to be established and people were still talking in 1955 of the anxieties of those days. In 1954, a full Government report was issued in an attempt to disentangle the complicated strands of the background to these events. The investigation showed clearly that in the middle of the twentieth century politics and religion, secular and theological thinking were, for religious fanatics, still inseparable. The tradition-bound clerics demanded that even the least of secular functions conform to tradition, long sanctioned by custom, consensus, theological authority, religious decision "*fetwà*." Yet, they forgot, or never had realized, that much of what is popularly thought to have been established in the very earliest Islamic times, or supposed to rest on the "Way" of the Prophet and his Companions, is actually only the result of an evolutionary process.

The Ahmadîyah movement, against which the attack was directed, is one of the youngest religious groups to have emerged in Islam. For the traditional Muslim, its most essential point of divergence from Sunnî Islam is its insistence that Muhammad was not the last prophet ever to arise. The traditional concept of Muhammad as *Khâtam al-Nabîyîn* "Seal of Prophets" excludes for all eternity the rise of another prophet. (But does not that interpretation imply a limitation, if not a denial, of Allâh's omnipotence? The Koran itself calls Muhammad "Seal of Prophets" [Sûrah 33, verse 40], but a more liberal interpretation might hold that Muhammad confirmed, as if by putting his seal to it, the truth of all prior prophets and their testimony to the Unity and Omnipotence of Allâh.)

The Ahmadîyah sect was founded, towards the end of the nineteenth century, by Mirzâ Ghulâm Ahmad (died 1908) who claimed to be a *nabî,* a prophet, and eventually proclaimed himself the Imâm Mahdî. To both orthodox Sunnî and Shî'î Muslims, this was utter heresy. With the founding of Pakistan, the state to be based, according to the orthodox, on strictest adherence to Koran and Tradition, the fight against the followers of this sect took on serious forms. The representatives of orthodoxy demanded that they be declared a non-Muslim minority. This was to deprive them of the privileges and rights of citizenship inherent in their being Muslims, including those of holding public office or representing their country in national and international bodies. This fight was most violently directed against Sir Muhammad Zafrulla Khan, the present leader of the Ahmadîyah, formerly Pakistan's Foreign Minister and a leading figure in world affairs. The dispute demonstrated how divergencies in the interpretation of doctrine could grow into a major issue of politics and government. Thus it was in the Middle Ages, thus is has remained in our own progressive and enlightened age.

The ultimate reasons for this interaction should probably not be sought in religion and religious emotions as such. In Europe, too, until the beginning of the modern age, religion was the openly avowed issue, while in reality dynastic and political power was at stake, often itself only an apparent motive hiding much deeper-lying problems. In the East, similar struggles and conflicts cannot, as yet, find an expression except in religious terms.

CHAPTER THREE

Creative Tradition:
The Theological and Legal Foundation

I.

Islamic development through the centuries offers a most striking example of "identity and change," the two facets of the historical process. Henri Frankfort's definition of the "form" of a civilization furnishes the best comprehensive characterization of Islamic culture as well: "We recognize [civilization] in a certain coherence, a certain 'style' which shapes its political and its judicial institutions, its art as well as its literature, its religion as well as its morals."

By its inherent character as a religion derived from revelation, and a society founded on it through the medium of one man, Islam was forced to evolve a principle that would acknowledge the inevitability of change from generation to generation, without depriving either the faith or its communal institutions of continuity in essentials. Amazingly, Islam achieved this without an established church or the infallible authority of a pope; by an evolutionary process, it sublimated the antithesis of identity *and* change into the synthesis of identity *in* change. The arbiter in this process was evolution itself judged against tradition; this, in its turn, derived its ultimate justification from the original revelation, or from its mouth-piece, the Prophet.

To achieve this continuity, Islam had to create a workable technique. Two factors in the situation of the Muslim community during its formative period after the Prophet's

70

death made that necessary: the lack of any system of law or legal code, and the territorial expansion of the Muslim empire with the concurrent necessity of integrating its heterogeneous population. After a few centuries, the creative process of evolving new forms for Muslim thought gave way to the authoritative canon of Muslim theology and jurisprudence.

When the Prophet died, the Muslim community was small in number and restricted in locality. Almost immediately it began to grow into the world religion that we know today. Muhammad himself had never dreamt of world-wide expansion or world domination. His concept of universality did not transcend beyond his own world; this included Arabia and possibly the Fertile Crescent and the Iranian borderlands, if the legends of his embassies to the Byzantine emperor, the *Kisrà,* and the Iranian ruler, the Chosroes, have any historical basis. In addition, he allegedly had contact with the Negûs, the ruler of Abyssinia, a tradition that holds an element of historical truth. But the Prophet did not visualize the diversity of races embraced, within a century, by the brotherhood of Islam, nor did he anticipate the vast expansion of the Muslim realm achieved within that short time. He probably would marvel, would he return today, at the variety of races and peoples that profess Islam.

His utter unawareness of the expansive power inherent in his new faith prevented Muhammad from considering such possibility and from making any provision for the chance of its happening. The variety of causes for this expansion, besides the driving force of religious enthusiasm, need not be analysed in this study. But even within the compass of his own vision and activity, the Prophet failed to see the necessity for an organization that would enable his community to carry on after his death; except for the Koran, he did not consciously prepare the ground for legal, social and religious organization of the larger Muslim community to come.

In spite of his genius, Muhammad was not a systematic law-giver, not even within the limited range of his original organization. The laws revealed in the Koran are decisions *ad hoc* made to fit specific cases. His social legislation is cut to the requirements of his own societal environment, for instance, the regulations affecting family relations, marriage and inheritance. They required, and later received, detailed elaboration to be adaptable to the needs of a much more complicated, diversified and sophisticated society. To create a system of institutions and a code of law was the task that confronted the generations following Muhammad.. They had to meet the needs of the expanding Muslim society, with its changing and widening social and religious outlook; still, they had to remain true to the fundamental principles of Islam. The scholars evolved a method which, though probably not entirely uninfluenced by earlier example, became, in extent and refinement of technique, peculiar to Islam.

During the Prophet's lifetime, his followers had free access to him for advice, judgement and decision, a method of governing that the late king Ibn Sa'ûd emulated in his Arabian desert kingdom. Muhammad's emissaries to the Arab tribes outside Mecca and Medînah received instructions regarding the teaching of the essentials of Islam, the Koran, the prayers, and the principle of the alms tax, to new converts; but in unforeseen situations and in the absence of definite rulings, they had to use their own judgement and to fashion decisions in analogy to known actions and attitudes of the Prophet's. The latter became the ideal example for conduct in Islam. The quest for knowledge of Muhammad's stand increased with his death, and the reports of eyewitnesses in his entourage, the "Companions," were elicited and collected; these reports gradually acquired great weight and authority.

With the passing of time, the collection of eyewitness accounts became systematic; the death of Muhammad's own contemporaries made it necessary to rely on second-hand reports by their sons, later those of their grandsons. Eventually chains of transmitters developed that bridged the gap between the living generation and the Prophet's age in which each scholar would refer to an earlier authority from which he had heard the tale. *Hadîth,* the Arabic word for "tale," became the technical term for these reports as well as for the resulting theological system. If these "Traditions" (the conventional western equivalent for *Hadith*) were to be accepted as reliable, the transmitting authorities had to have an acknowledged reputation for trustworthiness and scholarship. In Muslim eyes, the reliability of the authorities vouched for the truth of the report.

In this manner, later generations believed to have trustworthy information about the customs and manners, the "way of life" in the Prophet's own lifetime; for the descendants, *Hadith* embodied the "Way" of the Prophet. That is the meaning of the term *Sunnah*; for the Muslim it acquired binding force. In our day, it is the banner round which the orthodox rally and their watchword against reform; as such, it has become familiar, even attained a certain notoriety, in non-Muslim circles. In this way, the continuity of Islamic pattern of thought, attitudes and actions was, and still is, held assured.

With the widening intellectual horizon, coinciding with the territorial expansion of the empire and, at least partially, caused by it, the problems to be coped with covered an ever-widening range. They touched every aspect of the Islamic way of life and concerned in detail the "allowed and forbidden," that is, the minutiae of its ritual, its religious and secular practice. They ranged, too, over its whole intellectual, spiritual, and philosophic field. In the course of this development, *Hadith* assumed a function far beyond the scope of its earlier stage. Instead of being merely the repository of past usages and traditions as a guide to correct behaviour, it became the instrument for introducing or repudiating innovations. Theological, philosophic, religious and legal disputes were fought by way of *Hadith*, ideas were proved and disproved by it. *Hadith* thus became a weapon in the hands of proponents and adversaries on either side of an argument.

This led to a most striking phenomenon, peculiar to Islam and probably not found in any other religious system. *Hadith* was no longer an end in itself, sought for its intrinsic value as a proof for the validity of actual usage. It was found to be an unbeatable argument in support of any action, thesis, assertion, or dogma that was under discussion or attack. If one could but cite the Prophet's example, the adversary was silenced by the weight of its authority, except, if he in turn could produce a Tradition showing the Prophet's opposition to the contended thesis. Once this disputation by *Hadîth* was found to work, the scholars began to search for traditions to prove every shade of opinion. In the end, if no genuine report was found to bear out one's point, some tale was invented to be used as proof in the dispute and was provided with an imposing array of authorities to proclaim its authenticity. Eventually, the intellectual movements in Islam fought their battles over dogmatic, philosophic or religious differences armed with the weapon of *Hadîth*; the Prophet's *Sunnah* "Way of action and opinion" was invoked to prove argument and counterargument.

Gradually, such a vast number of alleged *Hadîth* of the Prophet's accumulated that the Muslims themselves had to find means of separating the grain from the chaff. They resorted to investigating the trustworthiness of the supporting authorities in the chain of transmitters. If these were found unreliable, if any link in the chain of authorities was defect or suspect, the report itself did not command belief and was discarded as unauthentic. With it, the opinion it purported to uphold was rejected as unacceptable, unless it was supported elsewhere by "sound" tradition. The six canonical collections of *Hadîth*, which became authoritative and binding for all ages, above all that of al-Bukhârî (died 870 A.D.), included only "sound" traditions, i.e., such *Hadîth* that had passed that test (though their authors differ somewhat in their standards and the severity of their application).

II.

On the surface, this method appears to be based on a conscious attempt at deception. Such interpretation would, however, misjudge the essential character of *Hadîth*. It was an attempt at upholding the continuity of development under changing conditions, at retaining ancient values while conforming to new approaches and fulfilling new tasks and obligations.

It enabled the Muslims to uphold inherited customs while adjusting to new insights, and to define traditional Muslim conduct in an ever-widening, ever-changing, ever-progressing environment. *Hadith is* "identity in change." It is the method by which those early generations, in the first centuries of Islam tried to solve the problem of continuity in spite of development, in a specific Islamic manner, so-to-speak, in "the spirit of Islam." It was recognized as such by those scholars that established the Prophet's *Sunnah* as a source of Islamic law second only to the Koran, i.e., Revelation itself; though it was not Allâh's own utterance, it was considered divinely inspired, reflecting Muhammad's own divinely guided judgement.

The process of elimination was not arbitrary; whatever was eventually accepted as binding, or rejected as contrary to the spirit of Islam, was submitted to severe tests. Established custom that had proved a benefit for the community and could uphold its validity before the court of "common opinion" was admitted into the body of Muslim law gradually to become binding canon law. Whatever was held detrimental to communal welfare, divisive instead of furthering common interest, or antagonistic to accepted ideas, was refused entrance into the canon and declared "bad innovation." Thus, "Consensus of the Community," represented by its scholars and learned men (*Ijmâ'*) was the arbiter for or against incorporation of a Tradition and the legal theory, religious concept, philosophic maxim or theological dogma which it upheld. The Prophet himself was invoked to give *Ijmâ'* his sanction, "for," said he, "my community will never agree in error."

If neither Koran nor *Sunnah* would yield any explicit ruling, intelligent deduction from analogous situations based on study, thoughtful interpretation and individual insight was permitted during the creative period of *Hadith*. With the growing amount of precedence and decisions available, this method became first suspect, as prone to error due to human frailty, then it was rejected as subjective, at last forbidden. In the beginning, research had been intellectual exploration of the merits of a case and search for analogous cases leading to new judgements

and decisions; henceforth, it meant study of Traditions and
Canon Law in order to find earlier decisions applicable to the
case under consideration. When the "door to free investigation"
(as we may freely translate the Muslim slogan *bâb al-ijtihâd*)
was closed, that is, when independent interpretation of principles ceased, creative development of Muslim law, so freely and
constructively cultivated in the first few centuries of Islam,
came to an end and has not yet been revived—at least not
openly and admittedly.

For the Muslim mind, *Hadîth* and *Sunnah* eventually acquired a sanctity second only to the Koran itself. The traditions embodied in the six canonical books—and some in other
collections of Tradition not considered canonical but held in
high esteem—were considered a true mirror of the Prophet's
thought. They may record an expression of his approval or
disapproval, or an act of omission or commission; they may reflect an opinion of his, directly uttered or indirectly suggested,
or contain an expressed or implied permission or prohibition.
The Believer considers canonical *Hadîth* to be a genuine, authentic record of Muhammad's reactions in various situations,
guaranteed by the authority of a knowledgeable contemporary
witness; the resulting laws, in the Muslim's view, are binding
for all eternity. When the Believer quotes a "Saying" of the
Prophet's, he is referring to *Hadîth;* the Koran, to him, is "the
Word of Allâh."

The non-Muslim looks at this concept with some amazement, especially when the study of *Hadîth* reveals a large number of contradictory reports proving exact opposites. This
amazement grows when the student further finds innumerable
"traditions" dealing with problems that rose long after the
Prophet's death or forecasting future events. The Prophet
who firmly declined to "prophesy" is, in *Hadîth,* alleged to
have foreseen dissension, factions and sects that rose many generations after his time. His judgement is invoked to settle
dogmatic conflicts and controversies that came to the fore centuries later. Ought we therefore to consider *Hadîth* a fraud,
even though only a *pia fraus?*

Due to the insight of Ignaz Goldziher (died 1919), a scholar of genius, this rhetoric question can be answered firmly in the negative. *Hadith* must not be considered, as does Muslim orthodoxy, the record of Muhammad's own time; it reflects discussions of contemporary problems as they emerged in each generation. Compelled to find solutions applicable to new necessities in a progressing world, yet aspiring to uphold the continuity of Islam, the scholars cast their deliberations as well as their decisions into that form. They demonstrated thereby not only their desire for solutions in accordance with traditional modes of thought, but also their ability to find them. *Hadith* and *Sunnah* are merely projections of contemporary problems back into Muhammad's own age. It was a way of expressing the conviction that their decision conformed to the spirit of Islam, that, had the Prophet been confronted with that problem, this would have been his judgement.

III.

This concept of *Hadith* is admittedly unorthodox; in fact, it was so strikingly new that even western scholars at first found it difficult to accept. However, it was soon recognized as a brilliant interpretation of a puzzling phenomenon; it has since become, without reservation, the basis for all western research into the theology, law and philosophy of Islam. For a Muslim, it would mean a fundamental change in outlook to recognize the truth of this thesis and its inherent possibilities for the present and future development of Islam. If the ancient method of free investigation (*Ijtihâd*) were re-established in present-day Islam, it might become the key to the solution of modern problems. The great philosopher and poet Muhammad Iqbâl was open to this challenge. Progressive Muslim thought may not yet be willing to subscribe fully to the validity of this western interpretation or openly admit assent. Yet its demand that "the door to free investigation and interpretation should be re-opened" implies a request for adjustment of Islamic laws and customs to the needs of a changing society and their re-evaluation in the light of modern life. That is, indeed, what

Hadith had meant in the early ages of Islam; the principle could be applied again to help modern Muslim society solve its problems of adapting traditional concepts to contemporary needs. Orthodox reaction is hostile to independent study and free investigation; moreover, it is opposed to any change in attitudes sanctioned through ancient tradition, and held sacred because the *Sunnah* is regarded as divinely inspired. It is the age-old fight of the letter against the spirit.

In opposing the "re-opening of the door to free investigation" the orthodox theologians refuse to acknowledge the creativeness of early Islam. For them, Islam has "entered the world as a rounded system"; nothing was added or changed without the Prophet's alleged sanction through his *Sunnah*. Because of its divine inspiration, all future generations were supposedly obliged to accept it without criticism of the whole or of detail. But the unbiased study of the history of religion with the methods of comparative religion shows that its forms are affected by evolution. However, the idea of evolution itself is not acceptable to the orthodox mind, whether in Islam or in Judaism. Yet, *Hadith* was in the past instrumental in solving the conflict between tradition and progress; indeed, *Hadith* and *Sunnah* are evolution. Through them, medieval Muslim theologians dared to face their contemporary problems courageously in the spirit of Koran and their Prophet. They had the strength to acknowledge the value of conserving the continuity while at the same time admitting the necessity for development and change. In *Hadith,* they had found the means for reconciling the two apparent opposites. In a famous tradition the Prophet himself was called upon to sanction this endeavour: "Whatever is transmitted in my name must be compared with Allâh's Book [the Koran]. Whatever is in harmony with it, originates with me, whether I said it or not." Thus, the newly created norms were related to the old-established ones; in the course of time, tradition and evolution merged to become "unchangeable *Sunnah*."

In contrast to the creative inquiry of the early scholars, modern orthodox theologians shun to admit that claims for

reconsideration of ancient solutions are justified; they shrink
from courageously attacking the problems in a spirit mindful
of the past, yet aware of the differing needs in a new era. They
do not feel strong enough to modify outer forms while remaining faithful to inner verities. In his craving for immutable
truth as an anchor for his faith and a norm for the conduct
of his life in accord with the eternal, the orthodox Muslim of
our day fails to recognize the subtle evolution of ideas inherent in ancient *Sunnah* itself. He overlooks the discrepancies
in the various positions supported by *Hadîth* and may choose
one alternative as the only one; or he may attempt, as others
have done before him, to reconcile the irreconcilable. The
living organic process of evolution is thus sacrificed in favour
of stagnation and dogmatic decision. But, says Iqbâl, "The
ultimate spiritual basis of all life, as conceived by Islam, is
eternal and reveals itself in variety and change."

IV.

This dialectic dominated the manner in which Islam developed and, in spite of its seeming opposition to change, is
still developing. It had its greatest impact on Muslim Canon
Law. Using the methods of *Hadîth* for its own purposes, it
equally combined reluctance to digress from the straight path
prescribed by Revelation and dependence on its authority, or
that derived from it, with courageous, forceful innovation. The
same powerful, decisive drive towards adjustment to new demands and the same desire for organic development were affecting the theoretic foundations and practical application of
the evolving Muslim law.

"Organic development" is probably the key to the understanding of Islam as a whole. Its seemingly tradition-bound
authoritarianism is in fact the realization that a sound society
must grow organically from firm roots. The early Muslim
who still remembered the social, ethical and religious integration of pagan times was conscious of the break with the past
demanded by the new ideals of Islam; for him a new soil in
which to take roots had to be found. For the emerging con-

cepts of Muslim law, as for every other aspect of Islam, that soil was the *Sunnah* of the Prophet.

From time immemorial, law was thought to be of divine origin. Moses received the Torah on Mount Sinai from the hands of God, *Themistes* were the god-given laws which the king received with his sceptre from Zeus (*Iliad* ix, 99) and Roman *Fas* was thought to be the will of the gods, the laws given by heaven for man on earth.

But law is more than the expression of God's will imposed on His people. It becomes—or, possibly, is in its very essence— the manifestation of the people's will to regulate their communal and social life by linking their sense of dependence upon divine guidance with their desire to fulfill His purposes for the benefit of their society. In Islam, the staticism of Divine Ordinance and the dynamism of the evolutionary process a- chieved a synthesis in *Shari'ah* and *Fiqh,* the practice and the science of Islamic Law, its jurisdiction and jurisprudence. For dependence on Koran and *Sunnah* did not make Islam as such necessarily "tradition-bound," static, unchangeable. The Word of Allâh, the Koran, Revelation, are the Islamic equivalent of the Eternal in every form of religion and ethics, *Fiqh* corre- sponds to its manifestation in their law. It is held to be the application of divine will as transmitted to a "law-maker" through direct contact with the Divine, by inspiration, by revelation, or "by seeing God face to face." Ibn Khaldûn, the great Mus- lim thinker, formulated this view already in the early four- teenth century.

Even the dominant motive in Islamic law, the connexion between social justice on earth and divine justice is ancient. In the ancient Egyptian concept of law, society and the god- king were inextricably interrelated. To quote Henri Frank- fort again: "In Egypt it was unthinkable that nature and society should follow different courses, for both alike were ruled by *maat* 'right, truth, justice, cosmic order.' The gods existed by *maat* and Pharao's speech was 'the shrine of *maat*'; what was right came to pass, in nature as well as in society."

Integration of God, nature and society is also insisted upon in the Koran. The theologians of the creative period of Islam expressed it, intuitively rather than analytically, by establishing four foundations of Muslim law, the so-called *usûl al-fiqh* "roots of the Law." It derived, above all, from the Divine Word, the Koran; the *Sunnah*, the Way of the Prophet, its divinely inspired interpreter *par excellence* applied it in practice. *Ra'y* "opinion," independent investigation of the man-made situation contributed the mutable factor, for it implied consideration of individual cases and arrived at decisions by fallible thought processes. To make up for that deficiency, that lack of eternality, the fourth "root" was necessary, *Ijmâ'*, the custom of the community as judged admissible by the consensus of its scholars. The timelessness of the ideal Muslim community raised *Ijmâ'* from being ephemeral and accidental to being the abstraction of the will of God as manifested by the "voice of the people." Ancient Egypt believed "in society's capacity of being faultlessly integrated with the divine"; Islam was convinced that Revelation had established integration between its society and its God.

In the creative period of Islam, dynamism was not feared; reflection about possible dangers came into play only after its creative impulse had spent itself. But reaction inevitably set in. The need for stabilizing the achievements of Muslim society created the demand for norms; these became more rigid the more their origin in divine pronouncement and derivation from sacred personality was emphasized. Independent investigation and free consensus of the community, in the creative period acknowledged as legitimate and necessary, were regarded as dangerous, subjective and fallible mass decision. The "door to free investigation and interpretation" was closed. In modern times, the demand by moderates and liberals for its "re-opening" conflicts with the fear of the orthodox lest, with the opening of the gate, the whole fence around Islamic law be destroyed and eventually the entire edifice of Islam collapse.

V.

The principle of eternal validity of divinely established law as such is not under attack even today, but specific attitudes and decisions are challenged and decried as outmoded by liberal minds. This fact calls for a clarification of the basic tendencies of Muslim law.

The most important of these has already been mentioned in passing. Social justice, the concept so much emphasized in modern society as one of the main principles in legal and social thought, dominates Muslim outlook, for the private as well as the communal sphere. No individual is allowed to act contrary to the welfare of the community. Whether in public or in private law, his right is limited by social considerations; in reverse, the community and his fellow men are bound to respect his rights and welfare. Al-Ghazâlî (died 1111 A.D.) even considers the principle of *maslaha* "common weal," that is, in his words, "the preservation of religion, of life, of mind and understanding, of descendents and property" as one of the fundamentals for legal decisions.

The direction of Muslim law is therefore twofold. Guaranteeing the Muslim's individual rights and providing the necessary environment for his personal happiness and well-being, is one aim, achieving the fullest integration of the mass of individuals into the social organism of the Muslim community, the other. Therefore, each person has rights as well as obligations, both in his private sphere, and in relation to the community. The latter has the right to impose on each of its members certain duties and obligations, such as paying taxes and carrying arms, for its benefit and continued existence; in turn, they are entitled to certain privileges as its members. The guarantor of this relationship is Allâh in Whose name, even at Whose bidding, through Revelation and Tradition, these mutual rights and duties are defined and executed.

Thus, in the last analysis, the welfare of the *Ummat al-Islâm,* the Muslim Community, is the premise for the well-being of every Muslim individual; but he must actively contribute his share towards its establishment and continuance. Far from being meek "submission," Islam demands ever-renewed action from the Believers; hence, the almost incomprehensible demonstration of tens of millions of people, in the face of well-nigh superhuman sacrifice, for the Muslim State of Pakistan.

Fiqh "insight" and *Shari'ah* the "path," guide him in his efforts by showing him which of his actions, in both the private and the public sphere, are useful or damaging, right or wrong, ethical or unethical, by the standards of Islam. In the words of Abû Hanîfah, the founder of one of the schools of Muslim Law, "the science of Law is the knowledge of the rights and duties whereby man is enabled to observe the right conduct in this world and to prepare himself for the future life."

The Muslim individual as well as the Muslim community (and thence, the Islamic state) regard themselves bound to fulfill their mutual obligations "under God." That is the deepest meaning of "theocracy" in Islam. But that term, so easily misunderstood and even purposely misinterpreted, denotes not weak, passive submission to the will of a god who, inscrutably, imposes it on society and demands it to be acknowledged as its law. In its flower, Islam had the strength to proclaim its conviction that Allâh was just of necessity and by definition; the dispenser of justice, He was Himself subject to His own demand. Though the Mu'tazilah, which postulated this idea in its extreme formulation, was only for a comparatively short period the officially proclaimed exponent of Muslim thought, the reactions against it, orthodox literalism and Sûfî mysticism, could not demolish it altogether. In modern liberalism, many of its tenets are discernable, though, as in Iqbâl, hidden in western philosophic garb.

In the balance, this mutual relation produces social justice in a community that, in modern times, has been so often attacked for its apparent social injustice. The Muslim feels a profound equilibrium between his obligations towards the community and his rights within it. One more aspect must be kept in mind: For the Muslim there is hardly any division between the religious and the secular spheres; the two are complementary and are variant expressions of one and the same verity. The laws of inheritance, for instance, in the legal concepts of other cultures not regarded as lying within religious jurisdiction, are in Islam strictly regulated by Canon Law. Marriage, on the other hand, considered by other religions a sacrament and often undissolvable, is, in Islam, a civil contract, not a sacred bond. Thus, *Fiqh* and *Shari'ah* elevate the apparently commonplace into the sphere of the sacred, but alleviate the religious awe in other matters by keeping them within the secular sphere.

CHAPTER FOUR

The Social Foundation

I.

In the wake of the Enlightenment movement, Europe and the West in general increasingly separated the religious from the secular sphere. A man's religion and its application to the ethical conduct of his every-day life are left to his own conscience as long as his actions do not go counter to "public morality" or public welfare. His activities are regulated by laws that limit the scope for gratifying his desires and impulses; but though many are inspired by religious tenets, most are not motivated by religious but by social considerations. In Islam, religion, on the contrary, encompasses man wholly.

Islamic society was shaped by this socio-religious ethic. From its very beginning, the Prophet's message called for social responsibility. The poor and the sick, the orphan and the widow were the objects of his solicitude. Allâh demanded of the Faithful social justice and care; in return, he was promised reward for practicing and punishment for neglecting it. The society of Medînah, being more complicated than the Meccan, presented more varied conflicts and required from its leader specific decisions, not merely awareness of social responsibility. The Prophet's response to that challenge as apparent in Koranic legislation still characterizes modern Islam.

In the legislation that Muhammad promulgated, in Allâh's name and as His spokesman, he strove for justice and fairness, for solutions that left the principle triumphant while avoiding hurt to an innocent being. This attitude is apparent in every one of the legal and human issues dealt with in the Koran, notably in the laws regarding women and the distribution of inheritance. The Koran reflects the deliberate manner in which the Prophet made his decisions after deep meditation, in Koranic parlance, after receiving a revelation. For that reason, most of the Koranic principles, if not the actual decisions, were able to preserve their validity to this day; though modern Muslims may wish for a modification of details, their guidance is not challenged. In the changing circumstances of the complex modern age, the exact provisions of the holy Book may not always prove to answer the needs as they did in the Prophet's days; their abiding validity in essence, for Muslim society, has not diminished. The task that confronts the modern reformer is to adapt the laws without violating fundamentals. But that has been the problem of the Islamic community ever since the Prophet's death; for Revelation had died with him for all eternity, according to the traditional—though challengeable —interpretation of the well-known dictum that Muhammad was "the seal of prophets."

It is necessary to apprehend the dual nature of the Koran as a religious and social document to understand the sincerity of those modern Muslims who affirm that it can remain the basis for the complicated mechanism needed in governing modern society. Muhammad regarded Revelation and the Koran as the link between the Transcendent and Divine and Allâh's immanence in Creation, the apex of which is Man. It is man's duty to fulfill God's laws in order to create harmony between these two spheres; this can be achieved best in society through an organization that complies with Allâh's deepest and most decisive demand: justice for all, pity for the oppressed and humble, charity. These are the tools that Allâh put into man's hands for his salvation. That man is responsible for his deeds and thereby for his ultimate fate, is a vital idea; though not consistently expressed throughout the Koran, it is essential for understanding Muslim attitudes fully.

For, far from being passive submission to Allâh's inscrutable will, Islam gives each individual the chance to contribute active-ly towards his own salvation. For instance, in the Koran

THE FOUNDATIONS OF ISLAM 87

slavery was taken for granted, in accordance with prevailing practice; but freeing of slaves was encouraged as meritorious. It was recommended as an expiatory act in sign of repentence or as an expression of gratitude for God's mercy and grace. Thus, the Koran, in the seventh century A.D., does not consider slavery an immutable, God-given state for certain groups of human beings, but an unfortunate accident. It was within the reach of man to ameliorate this misfortune. This consciousness of man's ability and obligation to fulfill God's will through society makes the Koran a social document of abiding vitality for the modern Muslim; this may amaze the non-Muslim, but it is nonetheless real.

The fundamental equation of religious and social ethics had its impact on the form of society that developed in later Islam. It determined the place occupied by each individual in it and by the various social groups within the commonwealth. From it emerged one of Islam's most outstanding features, its outspoken conviction of the equality of men as human beings. Economic inequality, with its concomitant social ranks, existed in earlier times as much as it does now; commensurate with a less sensitive public conscience, it may have been still greater. But almsgiving (*zakât*) is a compulsory religious duty, and an innate feeling of humility before Allâh compels every Muslim to look upon every fellow man as equal in His sight. Thus, to accept charity does not humiliate the receiver; on the contrary, the giver is offered an opportunity to do good for the benefit of his own soul. Poverty does not degrade the poor; the beggar in his rags can take his place at prayer in the mosque in the ranks of the worshippers with his head held high. Riches are a gift from Allâh imposing on the favoured man the obligation of sharing it with his less fortunate brethren. That is the basic meaning of the alms-tax, the *zakât*. Pious foundations, the so-called *waqf*, often established hundreds of years ago, give evidence of the discharge of that duty; some are touching reminders of the primitive needs of olden days, e.g., the *waqf* for offering a drink of water to the women who visit the shrine of Saiyidah Zainab in Cairo.

The West acknowledged the dichotomy between man as an individual in relation to his family, in his social relations, or as a member of a social or political organization, and man expressing himself in religious terms addressed to God. Such a distinction is essentially and inherently unknown in Islam. This basic difference between Western and Muslim concept makes it difficult for the Western mind to understand the denial of modern Muslims that an Islamic state is of necessity, or by definition, a theocracy, and for the Muslim to explain the difference.

The Muslim's repudiation is based on the definition of that term. In a theocracy, God would be proclaimed as the sovereign of the state, represented on earth by His vicegerent, the ruler. This idea is essentially un-Islamic; even the Prophet was only Allâh's Messenger, His spokesman conveying His message. Nor was the caliph considered Allâh's vicegerent, or the institution of the caliphate conceived as such vicegerency. The *Sunnî* definition of the duties of a caliph charged him with administrative tasks in a purely secular sense; he had, above all, the responsibility for creating and preserving the conditions conducive to the preservation of law and order, to the continued existence of the Muslim community, and, above all, to the observation of Allâh's laws. He was in no way a representative of the Divine.

II.

Democracy in the West is mainly a political term and refers to certain political rights possessed by every citizen of the state of which he cannot be deprived except by due process of law. It is identified with representation of the citizens in a body elected by voting, a democratic process in which the voice of each individual carries equal weight regardless of social standing, political or religious affiliation, race or colour. In the East, this concept of democracy is new and, thus understood, the term is imported from the West. But Islam aspires to a true, inherent democracy not based on the mechanics of voting. It never knew any differentiation between Muslims according to ethnic or racial origin, social standing or former religious affiliation. Within Islam "Every Muslim is a brother to every other Muslim," and Allâh Himself sent down the Revelation "Verily, We have created you of male and female, and made you races and tribes that ye may know each other. Verily, the most honourable of you in the sight of Allâh is the most pious of you; verily, Allâh is knowing, aware." (Sûrah 49, verse 13.) In the context of this study, it is irrelevant whether or not this verse is an interpolation by interested groups, as has been asserted; it reflects an attitude that Islam has always practiced. It is the Muslim's conviction that the state represents, to quote a modern authoritative work, "A divinely ordained system directed to the well-being of all men in this world and the next and based on a contract between the ruler and the ruled." For the Muslim, that statement holds good whether the ruler be a caliph or an elected assembly representing the people.

As the emerging society of the Islamic empire grew more complex, organization by groups developed, for more and larger ones had to find their appropriate place and their distinctive function within it. These had to be defined within the framework of Islamic principles. Each social group was allotted its defined place in the scheme of the Muslim community and later, in the state or states that formed it. A kind of *Stände* (guilds) organization emerged (as was common throughout the medieval world) which was fully elaborated later in the organization of the Ottoman Turks. Professional, religious and ethnic groups had their special quarters in the cities; remnants of these have survived in modern times. The well-known Bazaar of the Coppersmiths and the Spice Bazaar in the Muski in Cairo (the latter demolished to make way for improvement schemes in 1955), the bazaars of Damascus, Aleppo and many other cities, and the Jewish quarter, the *Hârat al-Yahûd,* in the Cairo Muski, also still in existence in the early 1950s, are survivals of this medieval organization. The newly proposed parliamentary representation of the Egyptian people by professional groups (in Ottoman times called *Tâ'ifah,* a term already used in the Charter of Medînah), though probably consciously modeled

on modern "fascist" prototypes, conforms to a certain degree
to the traditional socio-political stratification in Muslim countries; it had also been recommended as the ideal set-up by
medieval Muslim philosophers.

From the necessity to define the status of individuals or
groups rose the main division, still retained in the Muslim
theory of state, into Muslims as full-fledged citizens and non-
Muslims as its citizens. The non-Muslim world in general,
and the West with its different premise in particular, refuses
to understand it correctly. The "Contract of Protection" 'Ahd
al-Dhimmah defines the latter's status and guarantees the legal
rights and resulting obligations. Under the provisions of this
contract, the minorities are integrated into the scheme of the
Muslim state.

The Dhimmi, by definition, in Islamic law, is the non-
Muslim citizen of the Muslim state. Far from excluding him
from the Islamic commonwealth, the contract of protection
incorporates him by allotting him his rightful place within
its set-up; for the Muslim community can only conceive of such
integration and incorporation in terms of its own definitions.
The "People of the Book," that is, the holders of a revealed
Scripture, had always been held equal to the Muslims in respect to religious belief; dhimmah now defined their mutual
relation in legal terms. The word does not merely imply "protection," its usual interpretation, nor is it "tolerance" alone;
both terms have condescending and negative overtones. It is
a positive acknowledgement and definition of their status within the community, of their legal rights and basic claims. This
is evident, for instance, from the distinction made between a
traveller entering Muslim territory from abroad and the dhimmi.
The former was given a safe-conduct amân, comparable to a
modern visa, which guaranteed his safety for the period of his
sojourn in the Muslim region; it was, however, a temporary
permit limited to a specific period.

The world of Islam was not unique in having to cope with
heterogeneous masses that had to be integrated into its civic
organization and moulded into social conformity. It was a prob-

lem common to the Middle Ages that had to be solved in terms intelligible to medieval man. Nations and nationalism in the modern sense did not yet exist; empires held sway over, and at the same time, united, large expanses of lands with widely divergent ethnic and religious types of inhabitants. The Church which dominated the Christian world solved the problem of the non-Christians in its domain by giving recognized status to acknowledged group differences; by being set apart as a group, they were allotted a function in the social organization of the medieval world. Through the *'ahd al-dhimmah,* Islam similarly used acknowledgement of diverseness as a means of integration. Like the Church, Islam could express conformity only in terms of belonging to the religious fold; the contract of protection was an attempt, on the whole successful, to solve the problem of accepting "non-conformants" politically, while acknowledging their right to religious distinctiveness. It must further not be forgotten that, in medieval as in contemporary society, minorities were set apart as much by their own insistence in their differences as by the desire of the majority for their exclusion. Islam, in particular, has throughout its history been willing to accept the convert to Islam without reservation from the moment he had pronounced the profession of faith.

Partly through the Muslims' disregard for the tenets of their own Canon Law, the *dhimmi's* status suffered grave misinterpretations. Therefore, suspicion was frequently expressed that the exemption of non-Muslim minorities from certain obligations and their exclusion from certain offices, specifically that of head of state, would make the *dhimmi* a second-class citizen. This concept overlooks important aspects: The treaty of protection is an integral part of Muslim Canon Law (*shari'ah*) which in the medieval Muslim state dominated every sphere of life. It was so-to-speak the charter which regulated the *dhimmi's* relation to the Muslim and determined his rights and duties in the Islamic state. While the latter were limited in certain respects (f.i., non-Muslims were not called to arms), this charter guarantees the rights within its purview; the disabilities were not arbitrary but legally defined and counter-balanced by lesser obligations. It cannot be denied that in the course of history infringements against the provisions of the charter happened, but they were, in principle, a sin and a crime against Canon Law.

The delineation and legitimization of the rights and obligations of minorities passed through three stages: the provisions of the Charter of Medînah, the so-called "Treaty of 'Umar," allegedly concluded with the Christian and Jewish inhabitants of Jerusalem at the time of the Conquest (638 A.D.), and the 'ahd al-dhimmah resulting from it. Though the Treaty of 'Umar is spurious and the attribution of detailed special provisions for minorities to the second caliph chronologically premature, the traditions about it reflect actual conditions and its provisions were in force by the eighth century A.D. Viewed within its medieval context the importance of the charter of protection does not lie in the prohibitions and restrictions imposed, but in the rights and liberties left unimpaired or, tacitly or by implication, confirmed. To evaluate the institution of *dhimmah* only by its negative components, is to distort its true import. It is far more essential to realize that it leaves the communal life of the non-Muslims intact, upholds their religious freedom, guarantees them security for their persons and property and protects them from criminal and illegal attack.

In this manner, the non-Muslims were treated and regarded as integral constituents of the empire; their relations with other groups and with the authorities had a legal basis not subject to official or individual whims and prejudices. Canon Law which regulated every aspect of Muslim life, extended to these relations. Any infringement, any restriction, and especially the stringent and often malicious ordinances and edicts of later caliphs defied it; they were to that extent uncanonical and criminal, and never remained in effect for long periods. In actual fact, *dhimmîs,* both Jews and Christians, played an important role in various functions and capacities; they were bankers, viziers, physicians. Maimonides (died 1204 A.D.), the great Jewish scholar whose teachings are still binding for the

Jews of the twentieth century, was court physician to Saladdin
and his son al-Fadl. In spite of Bar Hebraeus' (died 1286 A.D.)
complaints in his *Ecclesiastic History*, the excesses against non-
Muslims in a period of hundreds of years were far overshadowed
by their flourishing culture and financial standing. In all fairness it should be stressed that there were large and prosperous
Jewish communities in Arab lands; Maimonides who had fled
from his Spanish homeland to Egypt at the time of the In-
quisition, and Sa'adyah Gaon who was born in the Fayûm
and flourished in present-day Iraq (died 942 A.D.), wrote their
works in Arabic for influential Arabic-speaking communities
within the Muslim realm.

Analysis of outbursts against the non-Muslims in the course
of history shows that they were caused by material, not by
religious factors. Non-Muslims were frequently economically
better off than the corresponding Muslim class; the latter resented their holding high office at court or in the administration
of public affairs. Muslim minority or sectarian groups, too,
often developed a higher economic status or set themselves
apart by better organization from the more amorphous and
less organized crowd of orthodox Muslims. The Ismâ'îlîyah
sect under the leadership of the Agha Khan with its well-
established social, financial and economic organization, or the
integrated and centralized social community of the Ahmadîyah
sect are modern examples. The wrath against the latter, culminating in the riots of 1953 in the Punjab, was expressed in
religious terms, but it was at least partially caused by jealousy
of their achievements through their social coordination.

Modern Islamic states find it difficult to make the transition from defining their statehood exclusively in religious terms
to that of nations in which religion is not the only criterion
for full integration. But it took centuries for the West to
accept that idea; it is barely a century since the first Jew could
take up his seat as a Member of Parliament in Britain, for
only since 1858 was a Jew allowed to take the oath, on entering
that body, in Jewish, not Christian, religious terms.

III.

Medieval Islamic theory divided the world into two camps, the "Abode of Islam" *Dâr al-Islâm,* and the non-Muslim world, called "Abode of War" *Dâr al-Harb.* The former were the regions in which Islam held sovereignty as a religious and secular power; the latter were, in theory, to be conquered for Islam by *jihâd,* that is, if necessary, by force of arms. These medieval terms play a certain role in Muslim political theory and international law and are not generally understood in their true connotation; a more detailed examination of their meaning seems therefore appropriate.

The word *jihâd* is derived from a root meaning "exertion." This may be applied to scholarly study, explanation and administration of Islamic law, and to this day, the scholarly theologian and judge is often known as a *mujtahid,* that is, a man "who applies himself diligently to study." The Koran commends "exertion" against the Unbelievers but without specifying the form these efforts should take. However, forced conversion to Islam was explicitly ruled out, for "There is no compulsion in Faith," said Allâh. But soon after the Prophet's death, in the period of sweeping victories and conquests of vast territories, *jihâd* acquired the more specific meaning of war with the implied connotation that this war was "holy," fought for the sake and glory of Allâh. *Jihâd* narrowly escaped becoming one of the "pillars of Islam," the obligatory duties incumbent on every Muslim. In theory, the Abode of War is subject to conquest; in reality, Muslim caliphs and sultans have made treaties of peace and friendship and commercial agreements with non-Muslim rulers at least since the time of Harûn ar-Rashîd and Charlemagne.

Christian hostility exaggerated the importance of "Holy War" in the subjugation of non-Muslim regions to Muslim domination. Even at the time of the Conquest in the first century of Islam, actual fighting played a comparatively minor role. Most of the conquests were achieved by surrender and peace treaties. These invariably contained clauses under which the "People of the Book" in the conquered territories could retain their faith subject to certain, on the whole not too painful, conditions. The notion of "conquest by fire and the sword" does not conform to reality. "In the first place," says Toynbee, "we can discount the tendency—which has been popular in Christendom—to over-estimate the extent of force in the propaganda of Islam. . . . In the conquered provinces of the Roman and Sasanian Empires the alternatives offered were not 'Islam or death' but 'Islam or a super-tax'—a policy traditionally praised for its enlightenment when pursued long afterwards in England by a Laodicean Queen Elizabeth."

Even the "pagan" populations of the conquered territories were not put to the sword, as Islamic theorists postulated; they constituted the multitudes that embraced Islam in the course of the following centuries. These converts provide the best proof for the disregard in practice of the theoretical legalistic formulae.

Though frequently demanded by Muslim religious theorists and fanatics, *jihâd*, in the real sense, has not been practiced for centuries. Whenever it was invoked in the last few centuries or in modern times, for example in World War I by Turkey against the Allies, it provided a religious front for power politics. In the conflict between the Israelis and the Arabs, the Azhar *sheikhs* proclaimed *jihâd* against Israel. The emotional and nationalistic reasons for this action do not concern us here; but its theological justification was, for the Muslim, evident. Islamic theory imposed the obligation to reconquer any territory that had been wrested from the Abode of Islam by war or conquest. In that case, *jihâd* is theoretically compulsory and obligatory; therefore, in theory, peace could not be restored unless those territories had been reconquered and their usurpers vanquished.

Muslim legal theorists make the most of the obligation to carry *jihâd* into unconquered lands, the Abode of War, in order to turn it into Abode of Islam. At the same time, modern apologists point out that unprovoked aggression against non-Muslim countries and, in particular, attack without prior summons to accept Islam, is contrary to Canon Law. In effect, both theorists and apologists are doing Islam an injustice; the former are converting a religious theory into a legal obligation of religious practice, the latter seemingly uphold the validity of the principle by a weak defence. Comparative religion may provide the real meaning hidden behind this controversial concept.

The theoretical obligation to carry Islam into the lands not yet under its sway has its roots in religious thought, not in a craving for political and military conquest and power. It is anchored in the fundamental desire of Islam to bring the whole world to the realization of Allâh's sovereignty "in Heaven and on Earth." This would be achieved if He were acknowledged everywhere as the sole recipient of spiritual devotion and acclaimed as the Supreme Ruler. The belief in this double function can be traced to Near Eastern antiquity.

For the ancient Near East, the country, its king and its god were inseparable. The country belonged to the god; its king was his personification on earth. God, king and country were different aspects of the same principle. If this bond between the country and its god was severed, if the king was vanquished or its god deposed, its most vital force was destroyed. Thus it was in Egypt and in ancient Iran; in the Old Testament at least traces of it can be found. Islam proclaimed Allâh as Lord of the Universe; its ideological heritage from the ancient Near East forced it to postulate His open acknowledgement as God of the entire world. Islam had the task of uniting Allâh, "the Lord of the Universe" with His lawful realm, of bringing about the union between Him and the whole world. Only when that union is achieved will world peace and harmony between nations be restored; only then will all human beings and all races and nations reach perfect happiness. Only then will the dichotomy between the worlds of the Divine and the Human be removed. Thus understood, the demand for conquest of the Abode of War and for subjugation of the whole world to the House of Islam is no secular, political notion; it is an eschatologic, not to call it a messianic, idea. Indeed, Islam expects to reach that blessed state only at the end of time, with the coming of the Mahdî, the Islamic Messiah.

CHAPTER FIVE

The Philosophic Foundation

I.

Hadíth and *Sunnah* served Islam well in solving the problems posed by its religious and social development and the growth of a civic and political community. Yet the greatest question of all remained, facing the thinker, not the social or political organizer. Neither Tradition, nor Law or social attitudes could supply its answer. It concerned the essence of God, the core of every religious and philosophic problem which the thinkers of the world had been trying to solve from the very moment that thought itself began. That question gave birth to both religion and philosophy. The prophet and the philosopher equally searched for an answer; in principle, their purpose, finding the Ultimate Truth, is identical, but the methods of their quest determine the character of their attempted answers.

The difference lies in the categories of the human thought processes employed. For the prophet, the religious thinker, intuition and inspiration are the criteria by which to judge the validity of his approach; revelation will be the last arbiter for the truth of his result. The philosopher holds that the answer can only be given by intellect, reason, critical investigation; *a priori* categories will therefore form the test for the truth of his solution. The prophet feels his pronouncements to be securely and unalterably attested to by the existence of God, the very fact that he wants to prove; he is thus begging the question. The philosopher's search for proof by rational logic is far less secure, but for that very reason far more dynamic and creative.

Because of contradictions in the sacred Book itself, the conflict in Islam is not even solved indubitably in Allâh's Revelation. In consequence, the Koran itself could be used as an argument for and against the opinion propounded, thus increasing the scholars' difficulties. The only way out of this dilemma was offered by either apologetics or dialectics. The one reality that even the sceptics and rationalists accepted was the existence of God and the truth of His Revelation, the Koran. But after granting that much, the ways of the theologian and the philosopher parted. The former did not doubt these two verities; the latter, though not questioning their existence and reality, was sceptical to that extent that he wanted philosophic proof for them.

Three fundamental problems faced by every religious system, the result of the clash between religious dogmatic assertions and factual, material conditions, had to be solved. They concerned the essence of God, the existence of evil in the world, and freedom of will. But while it was difficult to find a solution for these problems, the basic conflict between theologian and philosopher rested in the process of their thought itself. The theologian questioned neither the infallibility of the Prophet nor the inviolability of the Koran as the Word of Allâh, nor the inspired authority of the *Sunnah*; he did not doubt that even contradictory and mutually cancelling pronouncements in the sacred Scripture held equally binding force. In some instances, however, Revelation itself was thought to have abrogated previous Revelation; some of its own demands had been invalidated when their fulfillment was no longer either feasible or justified, though both remained in the sacred Book —the doctrine of the "Abrogating and the Abrogated Revelation" *Nâsikh* and *Mansûkh*. To the theologians, as argued in many treatises throughout the centuries, Allâh's very ability to cancel an earlier revelation by a "better," later, one proved His omnipotence as well as His solicitude for the well-being of His creation and His repugnance to imposing undue hardship. "Whatever verse (*Âyah*) We may annul or cause thee to forget, We will bring a better one than it, or one like it. Dost thou not know that Allâh is mighty over all" (Sûrah 2, verse 100) is the assertion that upholds that principle.

The theologian endeavoured to reconcile the irreconcilable, to establish harmony between contradictory pronouncements. God is presented in the Koran as uncorporeal, not to be imagined in any form comparable to earthly shapes; yet, His hands, His feet, and His face, His hearing and seeing and voice are recurring in Koranic metaphors. The theologian interpreted these anthropomorphisms in the most literal way. One learned *sheikh* is said to have slapped his own thigh when discussing the verse from the Koran "On the day when the thigh shall be bared"; another famous orthodox scholar, Ibn Taimîyah (died 1328) demonstrated Allâh's "descending" by stepping down from his dais saying "Just as I am descending," to obviate any allegoric interpretation.

The most difficult problem, affecting man's destiny most directly and intimately, was that of freedom of will. The Koran itself does not help to find an unequivocal answer. For, according to the holy Book, God's will guides and directs the world and all His creation is subject to it. "He guides right whom He wills and leads astray whom He wills" (Sûrah 74, verse 34)—and yet, the Koran so often yearns for men to make the right decision, to choose the right, not the evil, path and be saved. How can man choose, if God has known and determined, from the beginning, long before he was created, whether he would be "of those guided right" or belong to those condemned? Furthermore, if Allâh's intention in creating the world was to create Good, and if His deepest characteristic was His desire for Good and His abhorrence of Evil, how was it possible for Evil to exist? These age-old questions cannot be solved by religion except by blind acceptance; nor is revelation as such able to give the decisive answer. Faith only defers decision or begs the question; those who rely on revelation alone for its solution often do not openly admit even its existence.

The Muslim philosopher, on the other hand, did not close his mind to the contradictions, incongruities and problems. He acknowledged the urgent need for their solution and, recognizing that it could only be philosophic, courageously attempted to find it. The principal tool for this task at his disposal was Reason, that is, man's innate faculty for coping with philosophic problems; he proceeeded to make constructive use of this instrument. He did not deny God's existence, rather conceived of Him in strictest monotheism. Even to attribute to Allâh eternal, inherent qualities, such as His being omnipotent or omniscient, was a denial of His Oneness, an acknowledgement of other eternal beings beside Him, in Muslim terminology, "idolatry" *shirk*. He equally refused to take the anthropomorphisms of the Koran literally; the verses containing them should be taken as allegories. Last not least, he declared God to be just, and this quality to be inseparable from the concept of His divinity, to be necessary, essential. Out of His justice, He desires the well-being and welfare of the world and therefore, He leaves man free to decide which path to select. God gives man the choice between Good and Evil; He does not lead him towards evil, but does not interfere once man has freely chosen the evil road though he had been shown the right way as well.

The problem of free will *versus* predestination was in medieval Islam, as indeed it still is, the most disturbing of all and the centre of both theological and philosophic quest, though their approach was different. The orthodox theologian did not permit any doubt in the truth of Revelation, in spite of its contradictions and logical discrepancies. The rationalists made doubt the very touchstone for philosophic knowledge and eventual certainty. In pronouncements such as "The first condition for knowledge [i.e., philosophic certainty] is doubt," or "Fifty doubts are better than one certainty"[i.e., religious dogma], they anticipated Descartes by many centuries. These slogans were a declaration of war against the blind acceptance of religious dogmas. Yet, these problems, as well as their attempted solutions did not constitute an attack on Islam as such. The philosophers fought against anthropomorphism, stressed the unity of Allâh, and emphasized His justice; they considered themselves perfect Muslims, in fact, better ones than those theologians and defenders of popular ideas who, to their mind, obscured the basic tenets of Islam, Allâh's unity, His incorporeality and His essential mercy.

The Mu'tazilites, the proponents of these ideas, were philosophers, not theologians. They were rationalists, sceptics, not blind believers. But they were unwavering Muslims. They had no intention to destroy, or even attack, Islam; their aim was a purer, more rational, more intelligible, and more philosophic Islam. Their inspiration had come from Greek philosophy which also inspired, through Neo-Platonism, their extreme opposites, the mystics. Though they were sharply attacked, condemned and persecuted, after having been the officially supported dogma through the reigns of three caliphs, their philosophy was the leaven that transformed the reactionary theology of their orthodox opponents into the "moderate," "mediating" theological philosophy of their successors. The effect of their efforts is still felt.

In fact, the problems, in particular that of determinism, are still troubling the Muslim; enlightened thinkers, an Iqbâl, for instance, influenced by modern science and new insights gained through it, realized the discrepancy between the stand of philosophy and its traditional unchallenged acceptance. It is unfortunate that, like his medieval predecessors, the modern Muslim philosopher cannot free himself entirely from the fetters of his belief in the ultimate truth of Revelation. This prevents him from freely exercising his power of reasoning to the last consequences. When he strikes against the barrier of his faith, he abandons reason and re-introduces religious certainty by the back door, relinquishing his hard-gained philosophic ground. Like al-Ghazâlî, Iqbâl finds refuge in a Sûfic, or quasi-Sûfic, "religion of the heart."

II.

The rationalism of the Mu'tazilah could satisfy only people with an intellectual bent of mind trained in the methods of philosophy. They had acquired that inclination through their study of the Greek masters, Aristotle in particular, whose methods they had adopted though not following him in all conclusions. But the masses of Believers were not interested in philosophic subtleties; they were longing for certainty and for a closer relation between the individual and God than philosophy could provide. They were yearning for the intimate relation to Allâh apparent in the Koran and demonstrated by the Prophet who had gained his knowledge of Allâh's Reality through immediate personal experience and vision. Philosophy with its abstractions and rational logic could not satisfy that desire; on the contrary, thought and intellectual exertion could only interfere with an immediate relation between man and God. Fulfillment of that yearning could only come from one's own soul. Direct access to the Divine Power was desired, without mediator, neither Prophet nor Revelation; the goal was to immerge one's self into the Self, in consummate union with Allâh. The philosophic basis for this longing could not be found in Aristotle with his logical categories and his postulate of the immutability of the laws of nature; the fundament was not even Plato, but Plato in neo-Platonic garb.

Sûfism, i.e., Islamic mysticism, became the very antithesis to philosophy. Islamic dogma or ritual were, for the Sûfî, mere stepping stones on the way to that fulfillment. For the mystic, the problems of Hadîth and Fiqh, of ritual, personal behaviour, legal rights or wrongs, of social and communal relations, had little significance, nor were those of philosophy, e.g., the problems of causality, of good and evil, of prime importance. The existence and the essence of Allâh were beyond question; the aim and endeavour of the Sûfî were not enquiry, logical, intellectual penetration, but emotional experience of the immediacy of God. The Sûfî was entirely self-centred, a-social, lonely, the extreme opposite of the ideal attitudes in Muslim ethics.

Thus, philosophy and mysticism, Mu'tazilah and Sûfism, were poles apart, much farther separated than were philosophy and traditional orthodox faith. Each of the three would claim to be true Islam without conceding to the others the exclusive right to speak for it. Orthodoxy accused both philosophy and mysticism of heresy and unbelief, of being outside the fold. But modern Islam, and already medieval Islam, as it emerged from this struggle, would be unthinkable without any of them. Orthodoxy needed the leaven of both philosophy and mysticism to be saved from stagnation and unfruitful introspection.

Various "mediating" schools of thought showed the impossibility of containing ideas and restraining them from penetrating even through the strictest barriers and from influencing even extreme opponents. This is particularly striking in the Ash'arite school. Al-Ash'arî (died 935 A.D.), its founder, had proclaimed himself an adherent of the most orthodox theologian, Ahmad ibn Hanbal; but his disciples developed a mediating trend of thought by accepting principles first taught by the Mu'tazilites, in particular, their dialectic method, though moderated, possibly weakened, by their desire to uphold orthodox dogma. Their pattern dominates modern conservatism; but the Ash'arite school is also criticized by modern moderates.

By introducing the personal element into faith, Sûfism, too, loosened the rigidity of orthodox faith. This was effected by al-Ghazâlî (died 1111 A.D.), one of the most fascinating personalities that Islam has produced, one of the few Muslim thinkers who emerge as individual characters from among the frequent stereotypes. His inner struggle evokes a response in the modern western mind as it appeals to eastern imagination.

He had started as an orthodox theologian and a brilliant philosopher, an interpreter of Canon Law as well as an exponent of dialectic philosophy. He had held high rank in the famous Nizâmîyah Academy in Baghdad. At the height of his fame, he passed through an emotional crisis caused by the clash of the sterility of orthodox theology and the intellectualism of religious philosophy with the non-rational, personal attitude of Sûfism towards religious certainty. To solve this conflict, he resigned from his professorship and gave up all the honours bestowed upon him for his scholarship; he passed many years wandering in search of Truth, in search of himself.

This inner development is reflected in the titles of his two monumental works. "The Destruction of Philosophy" epitomizes his break with the casuistry of traditional law and the dialectics of philosophy; "The Revival of the Science of Faith" proclaims his hard-gained insight, after years of wanderings, into the essential need for the merging of faith, reason and human emotion. Not out of mere fondness for a play of words did the Muslims call al-Ghazâlî "The Reviver of Faith." The crisis of his mind mirrors that in Muslim religious thought and of religion itself, in his age; his personal salvation became the guide to salvation for Islam itself. For each of the three positions by itself held the danger of destroying Islam.

The theologians, by emphasizing the letter of revelation, endangered its spirit and exposed it to the attacks of sceptics. The philosophers, by their exaggerated stress on the use of reason, gave spiritual emotion too little share to satisfy human need. Last, but not least, unbridled mysticism, with its aim of *fanâ'* "self-effacement," its disregard for the rituals, laws and institutions of Islam and its pantheism, the opposite of monotheism, threatened to dissolve and to disintegrate the homogeneity of Islam and the community of the Faithful. Only a synthesis of the three positions, utilizing the positive elements in each, could save Islam ideologically. Al-Ghazâlî's creative mind produced this synthesis; he thus became the reviver of Islam, laying, at the same time, the fundament for future trends as well.

Al-Ghazâlî has been accused, too, of thwarting the future development of Islam by introducing the mystic element into Muslim philosophy. The modern Muslim thinker, led by his reasoning close to a break with the fundamental principles of his faith, can also take refuge in a "solution of the heart" and justify his stand by pointing to al-Ghazâlî's guidance. The more independent his philosophic thought, and the more familiar he is with the problems, solutions and laws of modern science, the greater becomes the temptation to save dogmatic faith by a flight into mysticism, or near-mysticism.

III.

Modern Muslim philosophy is trying to cope with the same problems and conflicts. In fact, the philosophic situation of today resembles that of the Middle Ages. Thought does not exist in a vacuum, nor are there any barriers to its spread or limits to the distance it can travel. In medieval times, Muslim thinkers encountered Greek philosophy and were stimulated by it into tackling their own perplexities; scientific research was also cultivated intensely and successfully. The modern age knows of almost no limits to intellectual intercourse and mutual stimulation between eastern and western thought and science, except the willingness of the thinkers to receive them and to allow themselves to be influenced by them.

Western progress in the sciences, in particular, has re-awakened the old questions; the East has not been able to remain aloof. It is therefore not amazing that the Muslim philosopher should be forced to take notice of the scientific approach to the age-old problems. The foremost philosopher in the Muslim world, possibly the only man in contemporary Islam who could claim that title in its true meaning, was Muhammad Iqbâl (1876-1938). His great contribution was his attempt to use scientific principles, in particular the laws established by the physicists of the twentieth century, in search for philosophic answers to the fundamental questions in Islam.

The most striking feature in Iqbâl's thought is the freedom with which he acknowledges the need for constant re-evaluation of the philosophic position. This in itself is no mean achievement and an unorthodox approach. As the sum-total of knowledge grows, as the scientific investigation progresses, religion needs re-examination in the light of the new discoveries and insights. For, to Iqbâl, "religion stands in greater need of a rational foundation of its ultimate principles than even the dogmas of science" (*Lectures*, p. 2). In this demand for rational investigation and full utilization of the results of scientific research, Iqbâl aligned himself with the rationalists of old. But his aim was reconciliation, for "religion can hardly afford to ignore the search for a reconciliation of the oppositions of experience and a justification of the environment in which humanity finds itself. That is why Professor Whitehead has acutely remarked that 'the ages of faith are the ages of rationalism.' " (*ib.*) This statement might almost be called programmatic; it demonstrates the task that Iqbâl imposed upon himself as well as the conflict which, in the end, he, too, was unable to solve except by recourse to what he called "Higher Mysticism." Indeed, he combined the position of the rationalist and the Sûfî; his problem had been that of al-Ghazâlî and at the end of his search he reached a mediating solution, as did the medieval thinker. Why that seems to be inevitable, constitutes probably the core of the problem itself; the philosopher's inability to find a solution as long as he takes the reality of revelation, the divine inspiration of the Koran, for granted and considers them unassailable. For, in the course of his Lectures, Iqbâl subjected other facets and aspects of Islam to a critical investigation and fearlessly reduced their claim to inviolability and infallibility. However, Revelation, the Prophet and the Koran remained the fountain and the arbiter of truth; they were, for Iqbâl, as they had always been, Truth. His belief in this Truth was the *canto fermo* throughout his philosophic discussion.

Yet Iqbâl was able to demand new modes of approach. "The task before the modern Muslim is, therefore, immense; He has to rethink the whole system of Islam *without completely breaking with the past.* . . . The only course open to us is to approach modern knowledge with a respectful but independent attitude and to appreciate the teachings of Islam in the light of that knowledge, even though we may be led to differ from those who have gone before us" (p. 97, the author's italics).

These courageous words promised unbiased, unfettered investigation. In a certain measure, Iqbâl kept that promise. He submitted the ancient, most vexing philosophic problems of Islam to a searching scrutiny in the light of modern physics, psychology and philosophy. He was equipped for his quest into the problem of free will with the arguments of advanced modern physics and viewed the age-old question of eternity from the vantage point of the theory of Relativity. But in the end, he used the results of modern science to support the traditional positions of Islam and he interpreted the pronouncements of the Koran with their help. Modern physics is thus pressed into service to prove the truth of the Koranic stand and Koranic verses are quoted to uphold the soundness of physics. Thus Iqbâl does not escape from the fundamental difficulty of any tradition-bound religious thinker—be he Jew, Muslim or Christian—of viewing the problems "in the light of Quranic teaching" to quote a Muslim's analysis of Iqbâl's scientific thought. But that is the equivalent of saying that he cannot sever himself from his dogmatic religious roots.

Iqbâl was freest and most forceful in his attack against the stagnation in Muslim social development through the fetters of *Hadith* and *Sunnah*. In no uncertain terms he condemned the statism that resulted from the "claim of the 'Ulama' of Islam for the popular schools of Mohammedan Law" and postulated unhesitatingly the right for every new generation to formulate their laws according to their needs. "The claim of the present generation of Muslim liberals to re-interpret the foundational legal principles, in the light of their own experience and the altered conditions of modern life, is, in my opinion, perfectly justified" (p. 168). This touched one of the most urgent problems in Islamic development, not only affecting theories, but live, practical issues; his intrepid and powerful stand for the "re-opening of the door of *Ijtihâd*" had, and will continue to have, great practical impact.

By declaring that "modern Islam is not bound by this voluntary surrender of intellectual independence," Iqbâl may have made his greatest contribution to the renaissance of Islam. For he became the undisputed leader of Indian Islam and its spiritual and philosophic mentor. Even his justification of this stand by a reference to the Koran cannot mitigate the stringency of his demand for a renewal and revitalization of Islamic practice and thought, though it is proof for the depth of his dependence on the Holy Book for justification of his stand. "The teaching of the Quran that life is a process of progressive creation necessitates that each generation, guided, but unhampered, by the work of its predecessors, should be permitted to solve its own problems." He endorsed the efforts of the Turks at freeing their nation from these fetters and greeted them (writing in 1928) as a sign of the "renaissance of Islam"; he demanded a re-evaluation of Islam's intellectual inheritance by "healthy conservative criticism," if for no other reason, "to serve at least as a check on the rapid movement of liberalism in the world of Islam" (p. 153).

Yet, Iqbâl with all his open-mindedness, with his thorough knowledge of western science, philosophy and psychology, and with his burning desire for helping Islam to get out of its stagnation and impasse, was himself constantly pulled back by the very fetters he was trying to discard. Nonetheless, amongst modern Islamic apologetic writings, these *Lectures* are like a breath of fresh air. Though he was reluctant to draw the last consequences from his own philosophic insights, he stated the problems unhesitatingly. He deservedly became the leader of progressive Muslim thought. Had he gone further, he might conceivably not have exerted the stirring, almost revolutionary, influence that he had on Indian Islam. He may have held back for fear of drawing the ultimate consequences of his thought; but possibly it was due to his awareness of the limits to which he might guide his unprepared people.

PART II

THE MUSLIM AND MODERNISM

CHAPTER SIX

The General Problem

I.

Islam thus developed steadily throughout the centuries; it followed a line of evolution that was determined by inner factors and necessities. External stimuli did stir it and roused its thinkers, often to provocative answers and unorthodox conclusions. But Islam was always able to cope with heterogeneous elements; it accepted the vitalizing and discarded detrimental and disrupting forces. Extremes were thus ruled out; but their stimulating effect served to strengthen traditional Islam. Hypercritical philosophy was mitigated by absorbing its creative ingredient, its dialectics, into the orthodox system; strengthened by that dosis of rationalism, it was able to overcome disrupting scepticism. Al-Ghazâlî made Sûfism fruitful for orthodox Islam by accepting its emotional personal factor; the latter's dryness and rigidity, its undue emphasis on doctrines, prescribed rites and rituals were alleviated by the Sûfî stress on "participation of the heart."

From this fusion, traditional Islam emerged revitalized; a middle-of-the-road position triumphed. Extremes of any kind could not survive except as heretical sects, Muslim all but in name only. Even Shî'ism remained within the fold and disowned its own extremists by characterizing as "exaggerators" *ghulât* those who exalted 'Alî beyond Muhammad and elevated him into an incarnation of the Deity. Islam probably owed its survival to this genius for moderation; for excessive rationalism, extreme mysticism and extreme Shî'ism might have destroyed it.

111

This ability to remain moderate, to restrain extreme trends and contain passionate feelings within the channels of ritual and ceremonial, is possibly the reason for the frequent characterization of Islam as a formalistic religion that is fully encompassed in a series of prescribed formulas, acts, movements and prayers at stated times. Nothing could be farther from the truth. Rather, it is an all-pervading faith that permeates all phases of a Muslim's life and envelops his whole being; the rites and ceremonies are only the external forms of a deeply felt spiritual emotion. In this faith, life and religion are inseparable; for the Muslim, Islam is life itself.

This moderation was not achieved without bitter struggle; it took centuries to crystallize. The discussion of the main problems of religious philosophy has occupied the Muslim mind almost from the beginning and continued throughout the creative centuries of medieval Islam. It was a sign of the dynamic strength of Islam, for it fell into stagnation and intellectual inertia only when that dynamism had run its course and when its political power, too, had been shaken. The vivid re-evaluation of its foundations and dogmas in the light of extraneous ideas and the philosophic disputation with non-Islamic thought in which Islam is engaged should be greeted as an indication of its regained vitality, not deplored as a symptom of approaching, or at least threatening, disintegration.

This debate is still in progress, it has not yet lasted long enough to have reached definite conclusions; the Muslim world has only begun to measure modern ideas against its own traditions and ancient philosophic and religious positions. Faster communications, intensified contacts and, last not least, the increased spread of education and the ease with which thought can reach the farthest corners of the world through the printed word and radio, have quickened the pace of development in recent times. Nonetheless, a fairly long period of assessment, introspection and adjustment must be anticipated.

Together with the victorious assertion of political independence, Muslim thought, moral values and social theories are being emphasized. Formerly, at least up to the early decades of this century, "modern," i.e., western, ideas were either repelled entirely or met with weak surrender—weak, because they were uncritically accepted as superior, or obeyed with resignation; today, "Westernization" is submitted to a critical analysis and only what appears to be valid, adaptable or useful, will pass muster. Thus, western technology is accepted as superior, on the whole, deservedly so; but even in the technical field it is realized that the applicability of specific methods to indigenous conditions must be submitted to a certain measure of critical appraisal. In the cultural and intellectual sphere, too, this scrutiny and hesitation, if not outright repudiation, is being applied. This is a sign of health, of new vigour and strength and a new consciousness of indigenous resources waiting to be tapped.

This reluctance does not rise from simple "anti-foreign" attitudes, sheer fear of alien ideas and foreign enticements and entanglements; even less does it originate in an innate inability to shed the fetters of ancient thought patterns. It is a re-awakening to the potentialities in their own world of ideas and in their own physical, especially economic and natural, resources. That this awakening should have its effect at present predominantly in the political and economic sphere is not astonishing; being tangible, these factors are more easily grasped and exploited. Intellectual and spiritual development is slow; influences in the world of ideas may remain latent for long periods before their effect can be felt and appraised by measurable changes. The world is watching at present the *process* of re-awakening and of fermentations in Islam; the span of time that will pass before the result will be ready for appraisal and judgement, or its eventual character, cannot be predicted.

II.

Again, as in the Middle Ages, the struggle within Islam is between the representatives of orthodox thought—the exponents of "unchanging, revealed, eternal Islam"—and the proponents of dynamism, of change by evolution. Under the impact of western ideas, the fundaments of Islam as well as their operation in all spheres of Muslim life are being scrutinized by both factions. Extreme alternatives would be either to abandon the old-fashioned, orthodox position, or to repudiate change totally. But neither alternative would be acceptable to the vast majority of Muslims who do not subscribe to any of these extreme schools of thought. For they desire, as in medieval times, moderation, adjustment, integration of new ideas, after due appraisal, into the proven traditional pattern. The moderates do not advocate uncritical discarding of tradition, but revision and new formulation in the light of modern conditions, modern achievements and modern needs.

The necessity of this scrutiny, consciously acknowledged by the intellectuals and their spokesmen, is also felt by the less educated who suffer from the conflict in spite of their inability to give expression to their feeling. Though often only half understood or felt as emotional restlessness or dissatisfaction, it permeates all strata of Muslim society. The young generation, in particular, realizes that there are new ways to follow, new problems to solve, new decisions to be made. They hear of the achievements of modern science, the changed outlook in social relations, family and community life. They want their own nation to keep pace with the fresh insights and desire to see them integrated into Islam. These youth are not irreligious, nor do they express dissatisfaction with their faith as such; they want to align the new with the traditional in it. But they often find themselves held back by their religious mentors who decry the demands for progress because they do not understand or admit the urgent need for modern adaptation. If the *sheikh* complains of the criticism of modern Muslim youth, he bears a large share of the responsibility for it.

The intellectual groups might be expected to feel the impact of this process of fermentation; but they have the intellectual and philosophic equipment for coping with the conflicts. It is moving to observe the deep effect on the common man. True, he will not be able to express his mental uneasiness, his fears or hopes, in abstract or even general terms. Progress, modernization, Westernization, liberalization, as intellectual is-

sues to be viewed in the context of nationwide and worldwide
change and dependent on technological and ideological movements, are far beyond his comprehension. Yet he senses the
existence of forces that he cannot grasp but that are changing
his world. He will talk about those factors that affect his personal sphere. He sees the gradual disappearance of time-hal-
lowed customs, the changes in dress, in the way of living, in the
rearing of youth, in the relations between men and women;
he becomes uneasy and disapproves of them. But the apparent
improvement in the state of those who adapted themselves to
the new forms makes him wish to share in their benefit. Thus
he is tragically torn between his regret for the vanishing old
traditions and his desire for the new ways.

The conflict pervades public and private life. It is manifest
in the simple every-day affairs, in personal and family life; it
forces humble men and women to face decisions that were unknown to their fathers. Even the fellah, so often represented
as ageless, changeless, by-passed by progress and uninterested
in political trends, senses the vibrations of that social revolution. The humble peasants suffer no less for being affected
only on a small scale; their conflicts concern their circumscribed
world, the upbringing of their sons and daughters, the tragedy
of their children dying in infancy, their poverty and helplessness
against vested interests. Fellaheen discussed with the writer the
problem of birth control in the light of the teaching of Islam.
They greeted Taha Husain's school reform of 1950 with enthusiasm and deep hope, for the promise it held to take them
out of their ignorance. And the most eloquent tribute to the
present rulers of Egypt the writer heard in 1955 came from an
illiterate farmer: "Now we count—formerly we were never heard;
we were as dust."

Nonetheless, the middle class hesitates to leave the traditional ways of life and to exchange the proven and trusted
familiar customs for the untested and unfamiliar. This is
especially true with regard to social tradition. The middle-class
farmer may adopt new methods in agriculture and use improved
tools; but to allow his daughter to attend school when she is

needed in the house or the fields is rarely even considered. This is not wholly due to ignorance or unawareness of the change in outlook; he fears to uproot her from her familiar environment and to make her unfit for the kind of life that awaits her. The sons of the middle-class urban and rural families are increasingly given an opportunity to acquire an education and to better their prospects; but the vast majority of girls has to be content with an education of the most rudimentary kind with very little chance for improvement in their social as well as their intellectual life.

The reasons for this fact must be searched for in social, psychological and religious factors. Muslim society is still well integrated; traditional standards are upheld and social strata continue to be well defined and respected. Family ties are strong, and trust, mutual help, and feeling of responsibility for one's extended family are still unweakened. Throughout the centuries, the family had been the safe refuge, and it has preserved that character. It provided support in every need, it was the reliable harbour to which to return in any emergency. How would one dare to abandon that security? The modern ways are suspect as a threat to that strongly-knit social unit; one fears to admit any innovation that might accelerate its disintegration. Opposition to any intrusion is, therefore, strong.

The orthodox theologians are the most resolute opponents of the forces of progress. For centuries tradition has stood unchallenged and established custom has not been disputed. External circumstances may have helped to smother creative or revolutionary impulses and, in consequence, creativeness was channeled into art, architecture, poetry. The Ottoman empire, with its strict, bureaucratic organization that accorded each person his place in the social structure and to each function a specific person, may have inhibited individual initiative; the result was acquiescence in the established order.

Even though in most countries the antagonism to reform or innovation did not take the extreme form of Wahhabism, the religious leaders and interpreters of religious law are not willing to cede an inch of the established orthodox positions.

They do not comprehend the motivating forces of modernism, since their intellectual equipment is solely derived from their compendia of medieval theology and, at best, of medieval philosophy; they are rarely familiar with modern scientific ideas, intellectual movements and disciplines, such as comparative religion or psychology, or they misunderstand and misinterpret them.

One of the greatest obstacles to reform is the strong emotional appeal of religion for the masses, as almost the only higher contents of their lives. But they are unable to distinguish between the essential and valid factors in their religion that ought to be preserved, and the ephemeral, the superstitions and the outmoded ideas that might be abandoned without danger to the essential faith. The latter often retard progress and could be discarded without invalidating the real religious values, those dynamic factors that are capable of development and adjustment to new circumstances and emerging new moralities.

CHAPTER SEVEN

The Social Problems

MARRIAGE AND FAMILY

I.

Modern man realizes himself most clearly in his social relations, as a member of his family or other group, as a citizen of his state or nation. Nations increasingly participate in international affairs and act as members of the community of nations. Modern ethics is therefore predominantly social. The individual is largely judged in his relation to society, his actions are evaluated in their effect on it; many, if not most, of the conflicts in modern life have their roots in social relations.

Many factors in Islam make the Muslim especially susceptible to this type of evaluation. In fact, the struggle in the Muslim world has its most deep-reaching implications in the social and political field. From the very beginning, Islamic thought and intent had been community-directed, its ethic social as well as religious; its religious resources are increasingly being drawn upon towards the creation of a vitalized, modern Islamic society. But before traditional ideas can be utilized to the full, some of them, in their present form retarding elements, must be re-evaluated and adjusted to modern conditions. In the individual as well as in the communal sphere, Muslim positions must be reappraised and certain features reformed if their traditional justification should prove no longer valid under changed circumstances.

For the Muslim, life traditionally moves in two spheres that have hardly any contact with each other. One, his family, is his personal domain which he guards jealously; he is its recognized master within the limits allowed by civil and canon law and personal and religious morals, and last not least, societal custom. The other is the world of affairs, of trade and commerce, profession and politics, of friendship and enmity; throughout the East, it is almost exclusively a man's world in which women have no part. In the Muslim East, these two worlds rarely mix; the separation of a man's private world and his active professional sphere is one of the most prominent characteristics of Muslim society. Even today it is still prevalent throughout the world of Islam, though its intensity is diminishing in proportion to the degree of western influence on the country as a whole and on the individuals.

Not every aspect of this situation is to be deplored indiscriminately; there are factors that exert a favourable influence, but others cannot but be judged as damaging and hampering national and individual progress and happiness.

On the credit side, both from the ethical and the social point of view, is the continued solidarity of the Muslim family. Even where the ancient institution of the "extended" family is dying out, as has happened especially in the cities, the relation between the members of a family unit is still very close. Blood relatives retain a strong feeling of responsibility for each other, marriages within the family circle are frequent in urban and all but habitual in rural environment. Inherited customs continue to be cherished and traditional ceremonial and courteous manners are cultivated, in spite of the increasing pressure of disrupting "modern" ways. The father's authority over his sons and daughters is still intact; in case of his father's death, the eldest son feels responsible for the welfare of his sisters and brothers, as his representative and successor in authority. The respect for the oldest and wisest member of the larger family circle is still great. These factors work for the coherence of a particular family group; they also teach its youth to acknowledge group responsibility and solidarity, and promote the acceptance of membership in larger groups with the obligation to consider their interests in all actions.

In the wake of modern conditions, this traditional attitude is beginning to decrease, for economic necessity forces men to leave their native village or town in search of a livelihood. Nonetheless, they retain strong group sentiments and remain conscious of the ties to their family and clan, (or as they frequently call it, "tribe"). The Palestinian Arab refugees are an example of the psychological effect of the disruption of such a unit by force. Apart from the obvious reasons for their cruel misery, the separation from their family or village group in which they had held recognized place and acknowledged rank, is the strongest factor in their suffering. Even in citified circles the effectiveness of this group unity can be observed; occasionally its exclusiveness may be relaxed and an outsider, not related by blood, such as a close friend or a visitor from abroad, may be admitted as a gracious gesture and expression of acceptance and trust.

While primarily directed towards one's own blood relatives, this training for responsibility also prepares for a role in the wider community. It is no accident that, in the Arab Muslim world at least, many of the most outstanding leaders—particularly those whose activities have been most beneficial for their nation in the social field, for instance, Taha Husain—came from a rural background in which that tradition was still strong. Not all these features are specifically Islamic; in variations, they are found in other societies throughout Asia. Islam has adapted and integrated them into its canonical social ethics. In its laws of inheritance, it continues to recognize the value of blood relation and family bonds by the wide range of relatives entitled to inherit from each other. That under modern conditions this inclusiveness does not always work as beneficially as it was originally conceived is due to changing social patterns and economic circumstances, not to inherent faults.

II.

One aspect of Islamic family life, in particular, has always attracted the attention of the non-Muslim world. It is the position of women and particularly the institution of polygamy. Frequently held up to derision and reproof, the intentions and implications of the latter have often been misunderstood and misjudged and were subjected to ridicule or to ambiguous misinterpretations.

The attacks came mainly from the West; but for some decades, Muslims themselves have joined in criticizing both segregation and polygamy. The western observer compared the status of women in his own and in Muslim society and reprimanded Islam for not giving them an opportunity to develop their own personality, as the West understands it; the material, intellectual and social dependence on their male relatives, and their political and professional retardation were criticized. The liberal Muslim was more reticent in his attacks on this traditional way of life. Raised in a society that, for a millennium or more, had regarded these customs as moral, he realized, in spite of western-influenced reservations, their assets as well as their drawbacks. The more thoughtful and sensitive he is, the more difficult it is for him to decide unequivocally for or against it. The advisability of abolishing the strict segregation of women, of giving them a good education and the right to vote and to enter professional life, is no longer disputed in many Muslim lands. But the Muslim rightly contends that men did not merely enjoy domination over their women, as western hostile interpretation frequently maintained; Islam had imposed on men great responsibility for them. The Muslimah's reluctance to leave the shelter of her family is based on that feeling of security engendered in her for many generations. Women were an integral part of the closely-knit Muslim family, with their place clearly defined, their participation in family affairs, if limited, welcomed and demanded and their position honoured according to their personal merits. Even materially, women had their share by right and were able to claim it as such. The West criticized time-honoured customs and integrated ways of behaviour from its own point of view. It judged from the vantage point of a society with entirely different organization and needs. Neither polygamy, nor segregation, as such, deserve the stringent criticism heaped on them. These institutions may have outlived their necessity and their justification. But the Muslim has to be convinced of their drawbacks and the West would do well to base its attempts at persuasion on Islamic, not western, ideas.

In order to comprehend the problem and the attitudes of traditional and progressive Muslim circles, a short exposé of the position of women in Islam as derived from their sources, Koran and *Sunnah,* is indicated. There are three major aspects, their personal status, their status in the family and that within the community.

The first aspect affects mainly the financial and economic position. In this respect, the Koranic attitude is astonishingly ahead of its own time and environment. It affirms the right of a woman to hold property in her own name and to dispose of it independently according to her own wishes. The holy Book allots her a share in the inheritance, both from her father's and her husband's property. In these provisions in favour of her right to personal property, the Prophet anticipated western legislation by many centuries. Thus, Muslim women are justified in pointing to the advantages they enjoy through Canon Law. A leading Pakistani lady whom the writer interviewed used her own experience as an illustration for the security of the Muslimah as compared with the humiliating situation of the Hindu woman that has been changed only recently. When she lost her husband, her inheritance from him was hers by indisputable right. Mme Pandit had lost her husband at about the same time; she had to plead (as told by herself in an article in the *Reader's Digest* several months after the interview) for some share of her husband's estate that would give her financial independence from his family. She eventually received it, but as a favour and by their grace.

Thus, even the western critic can agree with the assertion of Muslim apologists that Koranic legislation, on the whole, aimed at improving the status and the situation of women in Arab society of that time and that, in principle, it still has her welfare in mind.

Muslim family life, many adverse and half-informed statements to the contrary notwithstanding, is very close and affectionate. In all social strata, girls and women are loved and honoured and hold a secure place in the family circle; the often-stressed imbalance of a father's affection in favour of his sons is no more nor less apparent or customary than it is in western society. Only the Muslim's traditional reluctance to show his affection for wife or daughter in public produced this widespread but erroneous belief. Koranic attitude would militate against unfair treatment, for the Koran shows nothing but respect and consideration for them. Muhammad passionately denounced the cruel habit of burying daughters alive and a father's anger at the announcement of the birth of a daughter. He emphatically enjoined good, just and loving treatment of women and promoted specific legislation in their favour in various domestic situations. But the West points to segregation and polygamy as the two features that separate the Muslim East from it; they form, indeed, a vast chasm between them. They have, however, to be viewed in their historical development and from the viewpoint of their own society.

Segregation and veiling developed out of Koranic pronouncement, though the form gradually assumed was in no way demanded by the Koran. It became customary in post-Koranic times, after the Prophet's death. Nowhere in the holy Book does the word *hijâb* occur in the sense that it has acquired in the course of centuries. In the Koran, it is used for a "partition" dividing the house, never a "veil"; the *burqa'*, the garment that envelops a woman from head to foot, as worn in Pakistan, Afghanistan and elsewhere, is not indicated in it. Women are enjoined by the Prophet to behave modestly and not to flaunt their beauty. In particular, Muhammad's wives were reminded of their exalted status and required to talk to strange men from behind a "partition" *hijâb*. Only in the course of post-Koranic development, partly as protection in war-disturbed areas, partly out of social snobbery in imitation of the "Mothers of the Believers," were these recommendations accepted generally and did they acquire the character of binding laws; gradually they were interpreted as demanding complete severance of women's activities from those of men. Only then was "the veil" introduced with all the familiar prohibitions and personal and social restrictions.

The institution of polygamy is under attack even more frequently. Those who condemn the Prophet for allowing this custom forget that Muhammad restricted the number of wives that an Arab of his time could marry legitimately. Possibly, the Prophet introduced polygyny into Medînah and the Muslim community and continued to permit it in order to provide for the many women whose husbands (or prospective husbands) had died fighting for Islam. Both factors probably had some influence on the attitude apparent in the Koran.

Muslim apologists of polygamy and advocates of its abolition equally refer to the much-discussed Koranic ordinance on which plural marriage is based to this day (Sûrah 4, verse 3). But they emphasize that it ends with the statement "and if ye fear that ye cannot be equitable, then [marry] only one." This is held to express the Prophet's dislike of that institution and his preference for monogamous marriage. Owing to sociologic implications favouring polygamy that prevailed in his time, it seems doubtful that the Prophet really preferred monogamy; some of these are still in existence and are brought forward in arguments about the problem. But both attacks by Muslims against that institution and the attempt to justify it by Holy Writ are made on the basis of that Koranic verse.

In discussing its impact on Muslim society of today, it should be realized that polygamous marriage is only one of the forms that different societies may consider valid and legitimate unions. From the scientific point of view it is wrong to regard the monogamous form as exclusively right ethically and morally. In Tibet, for instance, the opposite custom, polyandry, still exists, in which a woman may marry several men, usually brothers. Different social and economic conditions in different societies have produced, in the course of centuries, these and other variants in the forms of, and attitudes towards, marriage. To the Westerner, brought up in the strict tradition of monogamy enjoined by Christianity, the decree of the Founder of Islam, in Arabia in the seventh century A.D., that a man may marry "one or two or three or four" wives, seems to imply licence. It aimed, however, on the contrary, at limitation of the number of legitimate wives. For before that time, apparently no limit had been set to the number of women a man might marry at the same time. Above all, it should not be forgotten that in Islam the second and following marriages are subject to the same ordinances as the first union was. They are solemnized under the same "Contract of Marriage" and are bound by the rules and regulations of Canon Law; all are equally legitimate and entail the same rights and privileges with regard to inheritance, the legitimacy of children and the procedure in case of divorce.

Nor must the decisive basic difference between the concept of marriage in Judaism and Christianity and that of Islam be disregarded. For the former, marriage is a sacrament, that is, fundamentally a sacred, indissoluble union; Islam considers marriage a social contract. It aims at establishing a family unit for the welfare of all concerned, the marriage partners and their offspring, but also for the benefit of the larger social unit, the state or the Islamic community. It is not without interest to ponder over this lack of sacrality in the fundaments of marriage as compared to the almost panegyric praise heaped by its defenders on the sacred inviolability of *purdah*. In modern times, however, polygamy is, to all appearances, no longer a vital factor for the Muslim community.

III.

The Muslim points to the principles of Koran and *Sunnah* as evidence that woman is not badly treated by Islam, even as compared with those in other societies, including, until comparatively recent times, that of the West. This argument is used in every apologetic discussion of her position by orthodox, moderate or liberal writers. The underlying reason for this apologetic attitude is not difficult to see. Western, and especially Christian, attack upon the apparent degradation of the Muslimah, has made the Muslim sensitive to criticism, but also aware of the measure of truth in the accusation. Nonetheless, he is reluctant to give up traditional custom that has, rightly or wrongly, acquired in his mind the sanctity of divine command.

The conflict is, at present, most pronounced in Pakistan where the old ways and the modern trends are clashing. The representatives of the extreme views to the right or the left, i.e., the unswervingly orthodox or the consciously radical reformers, have a comparatively easy stand. Unequivocally, the former assert the justification of the traditional custom, the latter assail and condemn it. In their firm opposition to any change in the laws based on God-given ordinance or divinely inspired Tradition, the orthodox cannot conceive of any need for modification; they are unwilling to discuss the problem and contemplate a possible solution except on traditional grounds.

The psychological difficulty and equivocality of the situation is most clearly revealed in the "moderate" position. While posing as open-minded and progressive, a "liberal" writer would attempt to prove that the emancipated western woman is leading an unnatural life, to the detriment of her health, her family life and her morals, above all, contrary to her natural functions. He would bolster this assertion with an impressive array of quotations from western authorities. Islamic laws and customs, in contrast, are extolled as wise, fair and just; they are said to protect the Muslimah from all those evils to which allegedly the western woman falls prey. However, most of the western authorities quoted, such as Havelock Ellis, Krafft-Ebing and others, or women writers, such as Mary Beard or Margaret Mead, speak of abnormal situations, maladjustments, neuroses and psychoses, or extol the happy state of primitive women in Polynesia in contrast to the neurotic modern female. Such Muslim writers further overlook that the drawbacks in the western way of life in general, and that of western women in particular, are not due to "feminism" and "emancipation," but to social evils and upheavals, such as wars and their consequences, depressions, unemployment and other economic and social factors. They are fighting against windmills and bogies of their own imagination.

Except for a favoured few, the average Pakistani girls and women have been brought up in this atmosphere of segregation and rarely have had an opportunity to compare their own restricted life with the fuller, or at least potentially fuller, life of their western sisters. They will defend segregation and the wearing of the veil as a protection against untold defined and undefined evils. The western woman will point to her freedom of movement, the almost unlimited opportunities for education and vocations, the satisfaction in her professional life, the stimulating exchange of ideas with fellow students or fellow workers. Asked to compare this wide range of potentialities with her restricted life, almost exclusively passed among women, or at best, men selected from a narrow circle, the average Muslimah will avail herself of the well-known apologetic arguments and retreat to the position "It is prescribed by our religion, therefore it must be good; the institutions of our religion may not be queried."

This attitude prevails mainly in the strictly orthodox circles, but can be found, slightly modified and mitigated, in more liberal society as well. The impartial western observer and critic is torn between sympathy with much that is valid, and opposition against the way the system is upheld, in theoretical arguments as well as in practice, in spite of modern trends and conditions. The western woman, in particular, deeply aware of the rich life that she can live if she has ability, possibly also the strength to overcome certain inherent difficulties, regrets the waste of ability, creative gifts and intelligence that might be utilized for the benefit of the nation and the people. However, the sentiments of the western critic matter little as compared to the loss suffered by Muslim society. Under the present system, which exists in varying degrees of intensity in Muslim society everywhere, much is lost by not using half of its potential assets for fear of losing all it values highly. Turkey recognized this waste and acted accordingly; but, in spite of a growing number of emancipated, highly educated

women working for the benefit of their nations, most Muslim
countries have not yet followed suit, or at best only half-way.
The issue will eventually be decided by the reaction of Muslim
men and women affected by the problems in their own lives.
For that very reason, their personal attitude is of such importance.

Both polygamy and segregation have outlived their use-
fullness. In modern times, many of the economic conditions
that made them necessary do not, or at least need not, exist
any longer, especially the inability of a woman to earn her
own livelihood and the resulting necessity for her to marry.
To keep women in *purdah,* as is still the prevailing custom
in North Africa, Afghanistan, Pakistan and among Indian Muslims, amongst others, or even merely to deny them professional
education and work, means letting a tremendous asset go to
waste. In theory and principle, the advanced Muslim nations,
including Pakistan, have realized that loss and are trying to
eliminate the practice. But social attitudes and prejudice die
hard; they prevent the majority of Muslim women from utilizing their talents, skills and knowledge to the full, and make
the most valuable of them a prey to dissatisfaction and frustration.

A very important factor in Islamic family life is its attitude
to divorce. The large number of Koranic provisions and regulations concerning it is indicative of its frequency and importance as a social factor in ancient times. Again, the impartial western observer is forced to state that in this respect,
too, the position of Muslim women is neither as favourable as
Muslim apologists assert, nor as miserable as biased reports
describe it.

Divorce is abhorred (and countless "Sayings of the Prophet's" to that effect are quoted) but considered necessary. Canon
laws designed to reduce the incidence of an institution that is
considered undesirable, but not always avoidable, safeguard the
interests of the wife. Muslim law makes divorce a financial
burden for the husband, for he has to provide in strictly prescribed measure, at least for a limited time, for the support

of his former wife. The dowry, an integral part of the marriage contract and irrevocable property of the wife, is a weighty factor in the legal procedure. It is permitted and customary to pay only part of it at the time of marriage. In case of divorce, the whole sum stipulated in the marriage contract must be paid. The wealthier the parties are, the higher the dowry agreed upon had been, the greater would be the financial loss for the man. Under certain specific circumstances, the wife has the right to demand a divorce from her husband which he could not deny; but even in such cases, it is the man who grants it, the woman who is divorced. In some cases, she may have to forfeit her claim to dowry or other indemnity.

Under western influence, but in accordance with Canon Law, specific stipulations and conditional clauses may be inserted into the marriage contract to prevent divorce from becoming too facile for the man or too difficult to obtain for the woman. Regional customs and attitudes also have helped to change some practices. Thus, among Muslims in the Indo-Pakistan subcontinent, probably under the influence of Hindu custom, a tendency has developed to regard divorce as highly undesirable and all but a disgrace. Various Muslim countries have adopted modified laws, though within the framework of Islamic concepts; in consequence, slight local variants exist today in the interpretation and execution of the basic canonical laws. On the whole, due to the financial obligation that has more impact on the rich than on the poor, the former do not practice divorce as extensively as do the latter for whom the dowry is negligible. Many of the innumerable beggar women in the Near and Middle Eastern cities are such unlucky divorced women.

Muslim women sometimes assert that they have the right to divorce their husbands; that is not literally correct. It has become customary to insert into the marriage contract a conditional divorce clause, the so-called ta'liq. This imposes upon the husband certain obligations, violation of which would be sufficient reason for the wife to demand and be given a divorce. This safeguard is used in particular to prevent the possibility of a second marriage. But even then, the husband gives, the wife receives, the divorce.

IV.

Where does religious liberal leadership amongst Muslims stand in regard to these questions? At first reluctantly, but then with increasing conviction and urgency, their gravity has been acknowledged throughout the Muslim world by men and women of all shades of opinion and stages of progressive thought or western-directed inclination.

The liberal theologians, foremost amongst them Sheikh Muhammad 'Abduh, based their aversion against polygamy on the assumption that the Prophet himself had shown preference for monogamy by his demand for equal treatment of all spouses. That provision was understood to imply both economic and emotional equality. Considering the near-impossibility to achieve that impartiality, the Prophet was thought to have indicated his dislike of polygamy without prohibiting it outright. Though this may not necessarily be the correct interpretation, this stand reflects the ever-growing repugnance to this institution within Islamic society itself; modern economic conditions as well as a gradual change in intellectual and emotional outlook among Muslims have reduced the incidence of plural marriages to such an extent that they do no longer appear to be the foremost social problem.

The indications for a decisive trend towards monogamy are increasing. The respective advantages and disadvantages of the two forms of marriage are increasingly being discussed by responsible bodies and leaders of public and religious opinion. Influential theologians, such as the rector of the Azhar in 1950, have expressed their willingness to discuss the issue frankly and seriously. Civil and Canon Laws are increasingly being interpreted in favour of monogamic marriage, and judgements pronounced in the courts are intended to pave the way for it. The custom of *ta'liq* referred to above, in particular, is used for that purpose; it provides for immediate divorce, with full payment of the dowry in case the husband would enter into a second marriage.

For the deliverance of Indian and Pakistani Muslimât from the restrictions of segregation, it is regrettable that Muhammad Iqbâl was not able to relinquish his conservatism in spite of his liberal ideas and progressive approach to Muslim traditions in other respects. His influence on Indian Islam, even after his death, continued to be paramount in Pakistani thought. Had he come out for the emancipation of Muslim women, for the abolishment of *purdah* and for their full integration into the Muslim social and public organism, their struggle would have been considerably easier. *Purdah* with all the concomitant disabilities and handicaps might by now have become almost a thing of the past. But Iqbâl, possibly characteristically so, was not able to take that great step. In common with most Pakistanis, he failed to see that the attack is less directed against her legal position—which admittedly has some points in its favour and can be defended—than against the humiliation of her individual personality. Muslim defenders of the system unanimously refer to her legal rights, but are blind to the intellectual starvation and degrading position to which, generally speaking, they have condemned their wives and daughters. These men are equally oblivious of the loss to their national and social welfare. Unfortunately, in this particular problem, Iqbâl was no exception, in spite of his greatness in other respects.

So far, Turkey is the only country to have legally abolished polygamy; in 1956, Tunisia announced her intention to follow Turkey's example. In all other countries that have any contact with the western world, it is losing ground as an institution and can no longer be regarded as a dominant social feature. To this observer, segregation seems to be a much graver handicap to their development. For in more or less severe forms it is practiced almost everywhere, except in the official, intellectual and high society circles. A careful distinction should be made between official pronouncement or legal status, and custom and every-day habit.

But even segregation is gradually disappearing; the number of women who are leaving *purdah* or its equivalent and who are taking part in many capacities in national and international affairs is slowly, but steadily, increasing. Judging from the gradual disappearance of "the veil" in Egypt and other Near Eastern countries, it seems preferable to leave the abolition of this and other outmoded and retarding customs to an evolutionary process; a decree forcing it might stir up religious controversy and strife. It is indicative of the changing attitudes that, in some countries, the demands for monogamy meet with less open opposition than those for equal civil rights, for ending segregation, and for improvement in legal and intellectual positions.

Thus, in the approximately sixty years since the success of western women stimulated the emancipatory movement of those in the East, the latter have progressed considerably in almost every field. The first public plea for their emancipation had to be made by a man, though at the demand of high-ranking women; but not long after, courageous and independent women dared to speak for themselves. Now, six decades later, able and outstanding women from many Muslim lands speak in national and international gatherings not only for themselves, but for their nation in general. This is, indeed, an impressive, admirable achievement.

They have thus gained much as citizens, though that fight is not yet ended everywhere. Turkey has fully emancipated her women; they have the right to vote and can be elected to public office. Indonesia, too, does not discriminate against them officially. In Lebanon, they can vote, while in Syria, a minimum of education is required to attain that privilege. In Iran and Iraq women are still barred from the polls, though a possible repeal of this restriction was indicated since the Federation between Iraq and Jordan. In Pakistan they have been given the vote and are eligible for public office. Able women already represent that country in diplomatic and United Nations posts. In Egypt, the fight for full emancipation is still being fought; in 1956, women were given the right to vote by an electoral law, not in the constitution itself. There are other countries, such as Sa'ûdî Arabia, Yemen and Afghanistan, that resist change in every walk of life.

But the fight is on everywhere, and there is hardly any region where the struggle for emancipation of women and a change in her mode of life is not being fought more or less vigourously. The degree of progress attained varies, as does the emphasis laid on one or the other of the many facets of the problem. In certain parts of the Near East, veiling is no longer the most important issue, at least not in the higher and better educated classes; in others, e.g., in Afghanistan, Pakistan, and even Muslim India, the veil and segregation are still outstanding characteristics. The problem of polygamy has recently attracted some attention through a few widely publicized cases in prominent circles; though it is still practiced, mainly in rural and middle-class circles, it does no longer seem to dominate Muslim life as much as in former times. But segregation of women is still an issue throughout; in varying degrees, from absolute separation to a somewhat masked prejudice against "mixed" society, the dominant feature in Near and Middle Eastern life is its exclusion of women. High society, political and intellectual circles disregard this taboo almost entirely; but middle-class people carry on in the traditional way, often while paying lip-service to their regret of that custom. Frequently there is a discrepancy between official disregard and its private observance, as is found in Pakistan in spite of its official recognition of women as full citizens.

EDUCATION

I.

Three internal enemies sap the strength of most Asian countries causing much of the misery that tears at the heart of every well-wisher and lover of these lands and their culture and way of life. The Arabic words for them have almost become proverbial: *al-Jahl, al-Fiqr, al-Mard,* "Ignorance, Poverty, Illness." These enemies have to be combated simultaneously, for they are interlocked in a vicious circle. Ignorance prevents

the poor townsman from improving his earning power, it keeps
the fellah in his near-bondage and makes both unaware of the
danger to their health inherent in certain of their habits. Even
if they would realize that, their poverty would still prevent
them from improving the unsanitary conditions in which most
of them live and that endanger their lives. However, Islam as
such is not to be blamed for this, even though its alleged
"fatalism" has been accused of preventing its adherents from
attempting to improve their condition.

That interrelation makes it necessary to discuss the question
of education in the chapter dealing with the social problems.
For only through better education will the common man realize
his precarious situation and understand that improvement is
possible once he has acquired the tools for it. In most parts of
Europe and North America, general elementary education has
long been obligatory and the accepted norm; illiteracy has been
almost eradicated or exists only in some backwaters. The average
Englishman, Frenchman or American of our day can hardly
imagine what illiteracy means. We demand *better* schools, *better*
teachers, *better* education—but there *are* schools, there *are* teachers, there *is* education for the masses. In the East however,
80 to 85 per cent of the population are still illiterate; schools
cannot be taken for granted nor is school attendance everywhere
an obligation and non-compliance with it a punishable mis-
demeanour. Under such circumstances, the whole approach to
education is different. It is not a commonplace commodity, to
be regarded as one's birthright. It is a privilege attainable
only by a favoured few. The writer will never forget the amazement, mixed with sadness, with which a young Egyptian boy
answered her question: "I don't go to school, I am only a fellah."

The ability to read and write, being rare, is admired and
lifts those who possess it above the ordinary level. The scholar
is a person of rank. The picture of the village children gathering around the writer watching her read or write is indelibly
engraved in her memory; nor will she forget the pride with
which one of her fellah friends showed her a prized possession,
a book on America which he could not read even if it had
been written in Arabic.

Educational and social progress are closely connected. Significantly, Qâsim Emîn, the author of the first book on the emancipation of women gave priority to demanding better education for her; he considered furthering her intellectual development a prerequisite to improving her position as a member of her family and the Muslim community. Similarly, raising the educational level of the people in general—for the vast majority that would mean lifting them out of total illiteracy— is the indispensable presupposition for improving their situation, their understanding of civil and political affairs and their participation in them. No wonder that intense use of the propaganda value of that problem is made whenever there is a political change; it may be directed against the parties of the government in power, it was also widely used in the fight for independence from foreign rule. Almost everywhere in Asia, the accusation of having neglected general education was leveled as a powerful indictment against the ruling group; neither indigenous nor foreign rulers have escaped from that charge. Any new party in power will therefore pay at least lip service to its dedication to raising the educational level; and the government of any newly independent nation will proclaim it as its most sacred obligation.

Yet, western educational facilities had been available for many decades. But they were accessible only to the well-to-do and were concerned mainly with secondary and higher education. Elementary and middle schools with legitimate educational aims of their own were neglected; school curricula were designed with a view to leading to university and professional training leaving the educational needs of the middle and lower classes almost entirely out of consideration. Only after the first world war did this outlook begin to change. As a result, there exists almost everywhere in the Near and Middle East and Asia a highly educated upper and upper-middle class in contrast to illiterate masses. Girls' education fared even worse.

II.

The responsibility for this is not to be laid at the door of Islam as such. Knowledge and education have always ranked high in Islamic, to a certain extent already in ancient Arabian, society. Pre-Islamic poetry indicates that the art of writing was not unknown in Central Arabia even before Islam. The Koranic revelations were written down almost immediately on being revealed. This, however, implies merely that there were a few persons who had acquired that skill; the majority of the people were left to admire it probably with the same fascination that it held for the Egyptian village children.

Islamic society accorded high value to *adab* "polite education"; but the feature of a sophisticated, refined and highly cultured upper class and aristocracy sharply set off against the illiterate, culturally somewhat amorphous, masses was as characteristic in Harûn ar-Rashîd's time as it is today. Present-day Arabs and Muslims point with justifiable pride to the decisive role their scholars played in the Middle Ages in the preservation of the Greek heritage. Far from having burnt the Library in Alexandria—a crime falsely charged against 'Umar ibn al-Khattâb after the conquest of Egypt in 637 A.D., while in reality it had been perpetrated in the fourth century under the emperor Theodosius—Arab medieval scholars translated the surviving works of the ancient Greek philosophers into Arabic, while Jewish translators worked on Hebrew, and Syrian scholars on Syriac, translations of the Greek classics. Between them, they saved many a treasure of Greek thought from extinction and oblivion.

The Muslim scholars built up on the fundaments laid by the great Greek scientists and made important creative contributions of their own in medicine, mathematics and astronomy. *Adab*, the "polite education" of the higher circles, comprised the study and perusal of the literary, aesthetic and philosophic masters beside creativeness of one's own. But side by side with the erudite scholar, the sophisticated courtier and rich lover of books and the arts stood then as today the illiterate proletarian and peasant. Even the highly trained craftsman and artisan of the East was illiterate then, as he still frequently is today.

The temptation is great, and has not always been resisted, to equate illiteracy throughout and unequivocally with ignorance, lack of information and slight interest in events not directly affecting personal life. That assumption is wrong. Even the masses are no longer entirely excluded from the stream of life; they follow, if remotely, the main events and sense the disquietude that has taken hold of their educated compatriots. This becomes especially evident by observing village life. One literate person in the community is enough to increase the awareness of its inhabitants of current affairs in their nation; world events are followed, at least as far as they may affect their own life.

Unfortunately, selfish interests and political propaganda are not above exploiting this dependence on oral and second-hand information. But political, economic and intellectual movements that may have an influence on its own mode of life do no longer entirely by-pass the village; they are discussed and appraised, and, if found profitable, welcomed. Two of the author's own observations that bear this out may be reported: Taha Husain's school reform of 1950 aroused rejoicing throughout Egypt's countryside; it was discussed by fellah and yeoman farmer in the villages up and down the land. A newspaper interview on the question of polygamy given by the rector of the Azhar referred to previously was discussed in the village gatherings with great interest because of its effect on the people's own life.

Even the poorest fellah observes the graceful courteous manner of traditional behaviour. His innate dignity is not apparent to the casual passer-by but reveals itself only to those who live amongst them. A simple gift, a tomato or an orange from the basket of a woman carrying her produce to market, is offered with a grace that honours the giver as much as the receiver. Literate and illiterate men rejoice in hearing and reciting poetry and many an otherwise uneducated Muslim knows the whole or parts of the Koran by heart. Storytellers in the cafés of the city and villages delight their audiences with the romantic adventures of ancient heroes and the highly embroidered tales of past history. Just as many a Westerner knows Harûn ar-Rashîd only through the *Arabian Nights,* the Arab

fellah will know him and other heroes of the past in this somewhat unhistoric, but that much more romantic and attractive
garb.

III.

Better education is recognized as one of the indispensable
means for helping these men and women out of their economic
misery. In this study, it is, however, viewed solely as part of
the problem of Islamic development under the impact of modernism. In this context it is an important factor as a major weapon
in the fight against retarding hyper-conservatism. As long as
the masses are illiterate and lack formal education, they are
cut off from first-hand knowledge of intellectual and social
movements, and therefore unable to take an independent stand
for enlightenment in their religion and for social and intellectual
progress. The religious leader in their community remains their
main informant, guide and adviser; rarely will he communicate
to them the debates, the stirrings of criticism and the misgivings
of modernists about the traditional ideas that prevent or slow
down improvement.

It was, however, fascinating to watch the gradual percola-
tion of at least some of these ideas into the lower ranks, in
spite of these handicaps, especially those that touched tangible
practical issues of every-day life. The rights or wrongs of birth
control in the light of Islamic teachings were frequently discussed in the author's presence by illiterate fellaheen or people
who, though literate, were too poor to buy books. Many topics
reached them by word of mouth; radio plays an ever-increasing
role in bringing instruction, enlightenment and propaganda
into every city, town and village. One radio in the village is
enough to exert good or bad influence on public opinion; if
wisely used, it might become one of the great blessings of
modern civilization.

The need for education of the masses is no longer being
questioned anywhere in Asia. This recognition, however, raises
the vital problem of its methods and aims. In the Muslim
East, in the last few decades, a twofold process can be discerned.

The first trend was caused by the external circumstance of foreign, western domination. Under its impact, the traditional, integrated Muslim scholarship concerned with topics and disciplines of its own religion-dominated search for knowledge gradually was relegated to an inferior place. Western learning and the curricula designed for western needs and interests were introduced to enable the eastern student to hold his own against, if possible to compete with, the foreigners. Gradually, the luminaries of western thought took the place of the great Muslim thinkers in the curricula of eastern universities. The founding of the Anglo-Muslim College (now the Muslim University) in Aligarh, India, in 1875 is the best example for this process. Sir Saiyid Ahmad Khan, its founder, had become convinced that the Muslim community in India would have to adjust its educational system to the requirements of modern times; without deserting the religious principles of Islam, their secular education had to be brought into harmony with that of the West and to follow a modern western curriculum. At the same time, the East was forced to compress the shift of accent from the humanities to science into a few decades, while it had taken centuries in the West.

The other change was internal. Traditionally, Muslim studies were concerned with religious and theological problems, and even the sciences, in particular astronomy and mathematics, were particularly stimulated by religious needs; modern outlook severed secular from religious disciplines. This phenomenon had a dangerous and disturbing effect. It separated those educated only in the traditional subjects from the westernized intellectuals. While formerly their discussion would be conducted on a level of equality, the western-educated scholar began to turn away from the ancient disciplines or to discuss them in western terms. Intellectually, these two groups did no longer speak the same language. A still greater chasm opened between the illiterate masses, uneducated even in their native learning, and the westernized intellectuals. Formerly only the barrier between the unlettered and the lettered man separated them; now they were alienated from each other by the whole pattern of their thought and outlook.

The educated Muslim began to live, intellectually, in two worlds. One was dominated by western philosophy, western science, western jurisprudence, western rationalism. The other was his religious, spiritual sphere. In varying degrees, depending on personal attitudes and decisions, he continued to adhere to the traditional forms, beliefs, rites and ceremonies prescribed by his faith. The faith of most educated Muslims is, indeed, as strong as ever: at some point, reason is silenced and faith alone allowed to speak.

The masses remained, on the whole, unaffected by this process; at most, they saw the slackening in the observance of traditional forms in the higher and educated classes and disapproved of some of the more extreme manifestations. The comparatively small number that succeeded in securing some minor job in a government or other institution posed another problem. Though in their own illiterate and poverty-stricken environment their scanty education and the small but regular income raised their status considerably, neither their financial nor the intellectual problems were solved. Not making much headway in their new environment, they became dissatisfied with both their former and their new life.

To that extent, education may even be a disrupting factor. The weighty problem of the aim of education is present in all "underdeveloped" areas, not in Muslim countries alone. Education should be directed towards all-round improvement within the native environment; the danger of alienation from the old circle and the unfortunate tendency to consider oneself above working in and for one's own groups, once one has acquired some measure of learning, should be counteracted. The Village Agriculture and Industry Development Progamme in Pakistan and UNESCO projects and similar programs in India, Egypt and elsewhere, are good examples of such integrated education of whole, organic groups.

The faith of these people is little, if at all affected by this low level of education. The *sheikh* remains their mentor and directs their minds. Almost without exception, they are literate only in their native language, and modern thought will not reach them except through diluted, often distorted interpretation. The urgent need for giving food to the minds of these people is only beginning to be realized; until recently the higher and better educated groups had been too preoccupied with their own problems and with the fight for independence to provide for the intellectual needs of those just emerging from illiteracy. But it is inspiring to see how much more is being done for the masses everywhere in the East than even a short ten years ago.

IV.

It is not the outlook of Islam towards education that has changed, but its contents. Islam itself has never been hostile to the spread of knowledge into wide circles. Fundamentally it has always considered learning at least a useful accessory to being a good Muslim and acting according to its laws and ethics, if not a prerequisite for it. Since much of Islam is ritual, and Canon Law regulates so much of its public and private life, knowledge is considered necessary for acting in conformance with their demands; it is an asset and a help, if not the necessary condition for it. Therefore, the study of Koran, *Hadith* and *Fiqh* is both an act of religious piety and intellectual search for guidance in one's personal conduct.

Everywhere in Muslim lands one can watch laymen studying, in the mosques, in their homes or their shops, alone or with a *sheikh;* they memorize a chapter from the Koran or Traditions, prompted and corrected by a friend (often the student himself cannot read). Should one call such a man uneducated because his education might be limited to such memorized knowledge or to reading his vernacular language, or the Arabic text of the holy books? All other learning, even any interest in it, may be beyond his scope and comprehension; yet, he is educated within the limits of his own world. His knowledge of geography, his ideas of the cosmos and the natural phenomena of the world, thunder, lightning, the movements of the stars, the moon and the earth, may be those of the medieval Muslim geographers and astronomers. Legendary Waqwaq of the ancient Muslim travellers may have more reality for him than London and New York (but it was a sophisticated Egyptian lady with a degree from the Sorbonne who asked the writer: "Do New Yorkers spend their summer vacation in Honolulu?"). Is such a man educated or not—literate, half-literate or illiterate?

This touches the crux of the problem. In consequence of Westernization, knowledge of Islamic subjects alone is no longer enough. The spheres of the East and the West have become so close that the Muslim no longer lives by himself, in his own spiritual and intellectual world. Indeed, that has never been wholly the case. In the middle ages, Greek and Hellenistic philosophy had deeply influenced the theological and philosophic development of Islam, and Taha Husain avers that, therefore, and for its Jewish and Christian heritage, Islam is closer to the West than to the East. Only the increased pace of development in the West and the initially reluctant intellectual participation of Muslims in it, after the stagnation of centuries, made the distance between them appear to be a discrepancy.

But the East is on its way to catch up with the West at least in scientific knowledge and technology. The integration into "Islamic thought," the conciliation and harmonization between western and eastern thought patterns will come in due time, and all indications predict that this is not too far off. There is also a growing desire in the West, born partly of political necessities, to increase its understanding of Eastern thought. Thus, East and West are moving toward each other, all appearances to the contrary notwithstanding. Once they have met intellectually and spiritually, and understood each other's motives and thought, their political rapprochement will follow.

ECONOMICS

I.

In recent decades, communication between East and West has been intensified, too, through growing interrelation in the economic field. Though widely acclaimed as a new development, it is the continuation of an ancient tradition of which scholars had been long aware. Mutual trade and financial interests, exchange of goods, sending of trade delegations from one region to the other, had been continuous from most ancient times. The spices of Asia had reached the West long before Islam had been born, and among the gifts that Harûn ar-Rashîd sent to Charlemagne were silks and a waterclock. Trade increased after the Crusades; but long before their time, the Muslim historian at-Tabarî (died 923 A.D.) records in his *Annals* the letter sent by Theophilus of Byzantium to the caliph al-Ma'mûn (813-833 A.D.) proposing to establish commercial co-operation between the two empires.

In the Middle Ages, just as now, commerce and the exchange of goods was truly international. All ethnic groups of the Muslim world participated; but many races of non-Muslim Asia also took part, Hindus, Chinese, Mongols. Jewish merchants and bankers provided the means of communication between East and West since they could freely trade in both areas. Thus, our own time only carries on the ancient tradition in commerce as it does in the intellectual field. And just as in our time the American business man may meet a competitor or associate from China or Japan in a hotel in Karachi or Baghdad, the medieval merchant mingled with those of all Asia in khans and caravanserais of the Near and Middle East.

With trade came techniques; the technological inventions of the Orient were carried from the easternmost part of Asia to its west and from there to Europe. Paper manufacture and printing from movable type had been known to the East long before they were known in the West. Indigenous arts and techniques were stimulated by eastern influence. The material and intellectual flowering of the Renaissance in Europe was, in no small measure, due to its flourishing commercial and cultural relations with the East.

As in the cultural field, the need for understanding fundamental Islamic attitudes in economics is great. The same tendency prevails of applying western standards and evaluations to conditions in the East and of using the criteria of western economics. This may be fully justified as regards the functional

causes for the high or low standard of economic and social
conditions. But the underlying traditional concepts must not
be disregarded.

Throughout this study, the specific Islamic attitudes have
been stressed; accordingly, here, too, the principles of Islam
regarding economics are to be shown. Specialists in this science
have fully analysed the prevailing economic factors of the area
and their effects, its poverty, feudalism, inequality of land
distribution, absentee landlordism, lack of industries. The premises, methods and results of that analysis, however, are not
primarily concerned with the specific mentality of that area.
They are applicable, *mutatis mutandis,* to underdeveloped
countries anywhere. But the peculiar ideologies of the inhabitants have to be taken into consideration, at least as a contributing factor. This is particularly true of Islam, for the
holy Book by which Muslims feel bound to abide, has laid
down specific rules affecting Muslim conduct in commerce and
economics.

The Prophet's observation of the Meccan business men had
given him an insight into the ethical dangers with which commercial dealings might be fraught if uncurbed by social conscience guided by spiritual motives. The social irresponsibility
and the covetous selfishness of some of the Meccan merchants
roused the Prophet's ire; the restrictions of the Koran with
regard to *ribâ* "interest" and profits from trade were the direct
result of the application of his religious convictions to the conditions of his every-day life. Jewish prohibition of usury with
which he became familiar in Medînah may also have exerted
some influence on his legislation.

The Koranic prohibition of interest has become common
knowledge. The often observed reluctance of modern Muslims
to put their money into industrial enterprise, e.g., in Egypt,
where investment in land is preferred, may be the result of the
psychologic conditioning of centuries against taking of interest.
On the other hand, the Muslim medieval merchants invented
a number of ways to circumvent the prohibition in order to
profit from business. Nor can the sad fact be denied that the

Koranic injunction against usury was only too frequently honoured in the breach; therefore, the fight of the Pakistani 'ulamâ' against the immorality of ribâ and their insistent drive for its official prohibition is not without justification. The Pathan moneylender demanding exorbitant rates of interest, the sarrâf in the bazaars everywhere, are abhorrent examples of the hypocrite who pays lip service to his religion but uses every evasion allowed by Canon Law to make his cut, without regard to the Koranic admonitions and heedless of the salvation of his soul. On the other hand, there are many pious men who take these religious injunctions seriously to their smallest bidding; but they are not those who attract the attention of the casual traveller or journalist.

The problem of ribâ "interest" has become of practical import in modern Muslim countries. At the beginning of our century, the question whether life insurance policies, dividends on investments or interest on bank accounts were permissible was laid before Sheikh Muhammad 'Abduh, then rector of the Azhar. The problem involved was the moral defensibility, on religious grounds, of gain without work, and of profit linked with unpredictable future events. 'Abduh's decision "fetwà" defended the religious permissibility of taking interest and paved the way for the opening of saving banks and insurance plans in Egypt.

The very fact that the head of that venerable institution could support any form of interest is significant. For, as in practically every religious problem in Islam, there were various degrees of severity in the application of the law, though the Koranic injunction is explicit and clear. These can be traced in the Traditions concerning the admissibility or prohibition of interest under various circumstances and on diverse kinds of merchandise. Those theologians who rejected the principle of "reasoning by analogy" restricted the prohibition to six kinds of goods explicitly mentioned in a Hadith from the Prophet (these were gold, silver, wheat, barley, dates, and salt). Others reasoned that these were representative example of types of wares; therefore they extended the prohibition by analogy to any product that might fall into these categories. Between these extreme positions were various shades of opinion and application.

The discussion on permissible and forbidden interest, reflected in the contradictory opinions expressed in *Hadîth,* serve to show the practices used to circumvent the religious injunctions in order to obviate loss and to insure profitable business. It is not without interest to note the comment of a respected modern Indian scholar of conservative persuasion on that matter. In his translation of the Koran, he draws attention to the divergent opinions and remarks: "When we come to the definition of Usury, there is room for difference of opinion. . . . Our 'Ulamâ, ancient and modern, have worked out a great body of literature on Usury, based mainly on economic conditions as they existed at the rise of Islam. I agree with them on the main principles, but respectfully differ from them on the definition of Usury. . . . The definition I would accept would be: undue profit made, not in the way of legitimate trade, out of loans of gold and silver, and necessary articles of food, such as wheat, barley, dates, and salt (according to the list mentioned by the Holy Apostle himself). My definition would include profiteering of all kinds, but exclude economic credit, the creature of modern banking and finance."

Medieval Muslims conducted international business on an extensive scale; they needed the means for carrying it on with a minimum of risk and a maximum of profit ensured. Far from being deterred by the Koranic prohibition, they invented techniques many of them still in use in commercial transactions throughout the world; the very names for them are derived from Arabic terms, such as "cheque," "tariff," the German term *"Wechsel"* (letter of credit) and others.

From its creation, the Muslim state of Pakistan was urged to incorporate the prohibition of *ribâ* into its Constitution. Initially reluctant to commit their nation, its drafters, in the preliminary deliberations, suggested to defer a decision for twenty-five years. The Constitution of 1956, however, accepted the inevitable stand for a principle intimately woven into the fabric of Muslim ethics, and proclaimed, in Part II, article 29: "The State shall endeavour . . . (f) to eliminate *ribâ* as early as possible." Taken at its face value, this seems to be an unequivocal stand against interest that should gladden the *mullahs'* hearts. But how early is "as early as possible"? Five years, ten, twenty-five, a hundred years—never? The Pakistani Constitution at every point shows a remarkable combination of statesmanship, legal training, moderation and religious conviction; therefore, the apparent vagueness coupled with a seemingly unequivocal stand against interest must have been premeditated. It will leave the legislators a breathing space to ponder the exact measures to be taken, the limits to which the prohibition should and could be carried without hurting legitimate national interests, the exemption from, and exceptions to, the law that may be established without contradicting Koran and *Sunnah*. It also will give the *'ulamâ'* time to study the traditional positions and realize how many profitable practices had been sanctioned in bygone centuries; they might consider the divergence of opinions that existed between the great authorities of Canon Law in the past. From such deliberations should emerge legislation that would neither be contrary to the spirit of Islam nor disregard modern economic necessities or hamper the desperately needed economic and industrial development of the nation.

II.

Muhammad consistently had shown an astonishing sensitivity to and awareness of social factors. The Koran emphasized the obligations of each individual and of the community towards the poor, the widow, the orphan and the handicapped. Allâh once blamed His Prophet for having been impatient with a poor blind man who had interrupted him while conversing with a rich and influential Meccan. Thus Muhammad's self-reproach at a trivial incident was immortalized in a Koranic revelation as a lesson for less exalted men and women (Sûrah 80, verse 1-10). This touching evidence of the Prophet's humility is not isolated. His own experience of hardship and the humble circumstances of his youth (Sûrah 93, verse 6ff.) had increased his sensitivity towards suffering of others. From this awareness rose the social legislation in the Koran.

From early Islamic times, part of the booty taken from the enemy was reserved for the public funds. The Koran made charity, almsgiving, a sacred duty, later to become one of the "pillars" on which Islam rests. It takes two forms, *Zakât* and *Sadaqah*. The former is an obligatory, fixed percentage, a sort of alms tax; the latter is a voluntary offering given as an expression of gratitude for Allâh's mercy, or as a substitute for involuntary non-fulfillment or violation of a religious obligation.

But most outstanding was the introduction of strict regulations concerning the distribution of property left by a Muslim after his death. The Koranic regulations still dominate the laws of inheritance in Muslim countries throughout the world. Possibly in this respect, too, the Prophet's own experience as an orphan and the memory of his dependence in his youth on the good will of his relatives may have led him to apportion an obligatory share in a deceased man's property to various of his close relatives.

Because of the fixed proportions due to specific "agnates" and "cognates," the application of the Muslim laws of inheritance is extremely complicated; it has been, from an early time, the subject of intense study. Being considered Allâh's law, it could not but gain acclaim. Muslim women, in particular, praise it because the Koran gives them a definite proportionate right in the property left by their fathers as well as their husbands and sons. The Muslimah feels her position in that respect to be superior to that of women of some other religions and nations.

From the purely economic point of view, there are certain drawbacks in that scheme. Koranic legislation, and its interpretation in Canon Law, started from a social order that no longer exists; it has possibly survived in some Muslim groups with an unchanged social organization, e.g., tribes that still own their ancestral lands in common and continue their ancient mode of communal life. Where the ancient foundations were no longer intact, the Koranic laws which aimed at keeping family or tribal possessions together, had the opposite result. Strictly prescribed portions of the major part of the inheritance must be divided among a large number of heirs entitled to their share; in consequence, the property becomes atomized. In Egypt, f.i., where land is the most common property, it is not unusual for holdings to be split up at the death of the owner; in a few generations the descendents of once wealthy land-owners may possess only a few acres.

That result is often held up to the non-Muslim as a sign of the social justice inherent in Islam. It is pointed out that these laws prevent the amassing of riches in one hand and pro-vide a constant turnover in property and wealth. The custom of the "extended family" is apparently a retarding factor in the process of "redistribution" and atomization; where it still exists, the advantages of these laws are underscored. But it is gradually decreasing and even where the closest family still lives and works together, remoter relatives who have a claim to a portion in the inheritance will exercise their right without remaining in the fold of the family. These conditions are, in fact, cited as a cogent argument against plural marriage. In a case within the writer's circle of friends, land that had been inherited jointly by half-brothers and sisters from a plural household had to be sold in order to distribute the shares in accordance with Canon Law. For this reason, its provisions, in spite of their advantages, may be at least a contributing factor in the all-pervading poverty.

These and other drawbacks to initially well-intended pro-visions of Muslim legislation have not escaped the Muslim jurists. One of the most fascinating phenomena in this complex of problems is the subtle modification traceable to western legal concepts in indigenous laws and juridical concepts of such Muslim communities as have been under European domination. British, French, Dutch jurists, or Muslims trained and admitted to administer that law, were obliged to settle litigations in which Muslim Canon Law was involved. But while taking full cogni-zance of the latter, they were applying to it the logic and modes of procedure, deduction and conclusion of their own legal systems.

In the course of time, their decisions, arguments and juridical logic became part of the legal equipment and mental processes of the respective Muslim communities; there developed a distinct Indian, Netherlands-Indies, French-North-African "Muhammedan Law." This applies to cases involving economic transactions, such as buying and selling, questions of interest, insurance of all kinds, wills and bequests, marriage and divorce procedures, in fact to all cases involving "personal" law. Though Islamic Canon Law remained its foundation, the principles of legal thought in the courts of the colonial powers became the basis for its interpretation, the way of argumentation and application. The result of that process became the accepted law of those countries and continues to influence their jurisdiction after independence.

CHAPTER EIGHT

The Political Problem

THE MUSLIM STATE

I.

Ever since the creation of Pakistan had been proposed, the idea of a "Muslim State" has held the forefront of discussion. Its theoretical foundation, its guiding principles and the possibility of applying them in practice under modern conditions were being examined. Since the French Revolution, the principle of the "separation of State and Church" has become the fundament on which freedom of conscience and of religion for all in many European countries is built. In the United States of America it is an integral part of the Constitution; it guarantees free development without interference from any religious authority and independence from demands to conform to any specific doctrine or persuasion. It has become identified with the uninhibited working of democratic government and is regarded as indispensable for upholding the equality of rights and obligations of every citizen, regardless of his religious affiliations.

The demand of the Muslims in India, during the fight for Independence, for an Islamic nation of their own was therefore received with considerable misgivings, even by those who hoped for its success. It was only to be expected that hostile opinion foresaw "a return to medievalism," with dire consequences for non-Muslims who were to live in Pakistan. The founding of an Islamic state in the middle of the twentieth century seemed to reverse the trend towards secularism in other parts of the Muslim world and to counteract the attempts at mitigating the impact of ancient traditions on their way of life. True, some nations that were governed strictly by Islamic law had survived, but they were labeled "relics of the past" and disposed of as "backward and still shackled by medieval superstition and beliefs." In western opinion, they did not really count, except politically, in the alignment for or against communism, or economically, as oil-producing countries; Afghanistan, Sa'ûdî Arabia and Yemen come readily to mind in that category. Yet, even the friendly observer could not help being somewhat apprehensive of the consequences of the decision to govern the new nation according to the standards of Koran and *Sunnah,* and anxiously followed the discussions in Pakistan's Constitutional Assembly on the principles by which the new nation was to be administered.

Muhammad 'Alî Jinnah, the founder of Pakistan, had dedicated the new country in conciliatory words to modern democracy and solemnly proclaimed religious freedom for all its people. For nine years, the finest minds of the nation, trained in legal, political and economic thought, worked for the execution of these ideals, often taunted by hostile criticism. On February 23, 1956, the Constitution of Pakistan came into effect. Mindful of their responsibility to their nation, their religion and all their fellow citizens, the framers of the Constitution had been trying to create in it a basis for its development and that of its citizens, without being untrue to either their religion or their democracy. The result of their nine years of labour, thought and arguments with antagonists within and without their own community is a remarkable document; in it, the sincerity of their religious conviction was blended with their ability to apply modern social attitudes and political democracy into a workable constitution for a modern state.

Its creators had to overcome in particular the unrelenting orthodoxy of the *'ulamâ'* whose mastery of the ancient texts was unrelieved by any attempt at rethinking the problems even within the limits allowed by Islam itself. For them, the "gate of independent thought" had been closed centuries ago never to be re-opened. But the makers of the Constitution grasped the true spiritual meaning of Islam; by applying modern political philosophy, social attitudes and legal principles to it, they created the constitution of a modern, not of a "medieval" state. The discussion of the principles of the Muslim state, in the *Report of the Court of Inquiry . . . into the Punjab Disturbances of 1953,* is illuminating. It shows, on the one hand, the unalleviated emotional obscurantism of the *'ulamā'* who had been called to testify as expert witnesses and, in contrast, the enlightened approach of the moderate, trained jurists.

Islam has frequently been declared inherently incapable of becoming the fundament for the formation of a state. A glance upon the political history of Islam should suffice as a counterargument. Granted, the Islamic *empire,* that huge conglomeration of incompatible, divergent races, lands, cultures and traditions, did not survive as a strong entity. But it seems that huge empires in general cannot survive for more than a few centuries. All empires in history have eventually disintegrated as political units. However, they developed a spiritual or cultural unity based on common interests; the emerging nations retained a community of ideas and a certain affinity of minds founded on their common past. The empires of Alexander and of the Caesars, the Holy Roman, the Islamic and the Ottoman empires, and the last, for the time being, in that line, the British empire, prove this.

Within the Islamic empire, nations had developed that formed the nucleus of still existing states; others were the precursors of nations that were re-created since the end of the first world war. Islam had been the religion of their state and, except for periods of internal strife or attacks from the outside, they had been able to hold their own among the nations of their time politically and militarily, as well as in trade, the sciences and art. The vivid intercourse with the non-Muslim world, both farther east and to the west, testifies to their importance in world affairs of their day. Their feudal organization, their undemocratic disregard and oppression of the common

man and the fellah may appall the modern historian. But in
that respect the medieval Muslim world did not differ much
from its western counterpart; medieval Muslim life must be
assessed against its medieval background.

II.

At all times, Muslim thinkers have studied the philosophical foundations of their way of life. The idea of a Muslim
state and the theories on which to base it offered the Muslim
a philosophic problem of the highest order. Two characteristic
attempts at evolving a theory of state, in particular, have become famous, the sociological analysis of Ibn Khaldûn (died
1406 A.D.) and the philosophic study of al-Farâbî (died 950
A.D.). Al-Farabî's theory of state is based on Greek thought;
but in its application, in spite of its Hellenic, neo-Platonic
roots, it is Islamic. Both Ibn Khaldûn and al-Farâbî were
thinking of the Muslim society of their own day.

The sociologist and the philosopher differed in thought and
method, but they came to a similar conclusion. The state is
the social organization that provided the best physical, intellectual and emotional environment for the fulfillment of the
fundamental human desire for happiness. This innate longing
of the individual is best satisfied in the collective happiness of
the community; its main purpose is to provide the best conditions for achieving it, to create the climate in which it can
best be furthered. In Islamic thought it had found recognition
in the principle of *maslahah* "common weal"; al-Farâbî as well
as Ibn Khaldûn accept it as the fundament for any community
life.

Ibn Khaldûn is the first Muslim to think in sociological
terms, that is, to consider man in relation to his fellow man
and to the physical, economic and social conditions of his
environment. The sociologist Ibn Khaldûn derived his theory
of state from reasonable, demonstrable facts, the philosopher
al-Farâbî from abstract philosophic speculation.

Ibn Khaldûn found the source for communal happiness in
economic and social factors, in the necessity for man to de-

velop his potentialities; each individual, by working at his distinctive task, contributes towards attaining that common goal. Urban life, with its varied forms of activities, its arts and crafts and commerce, offers the best social environment, for it is the highest, though not the only, form of social organization and civilization. Ibn Khaldûn contrasted it with the more vigorous, more virile one of the desert. Sedentary civilization is more elaborate, more refined, but the very factors that make it superior to that of the desert carry with them the seeds for its decay. Greater resources make for greater demand for luxury; division of labour leads to lack of all-round ability and to dependence on others. Inevitably, the cycle of rise, growth, summit and decline of a society is completed by the fall of the ruling class; in Ibn Khaldûn's system, that event is identical with the collapse of the state.

For al-Farâbî, the Ideal State (al-Medînah al-Fâdilah) represents the optimal combination of conditions conducive to a full community life. It is a "community of citizens striving to reach perfection by mutual aid and in true knowledge and genuine virtue"; this echoes the Platonic idea that the foundations of the state are wisdom, bravery, self-control and justice, which constitute the true Good and Beautiful. The greatest happiness attainable by man is highest perfection that carries him eventually, in al-Farâbî's neo-Platonic way of thought, to the sphere of the Creative Mind (Nûs).

Reflecting the neo-Platonic scale of values, the members of the Ideal State have reached these virtues in varying measure; they occupy a corresponding place in it and participate in various degrees in its creation. Its leader, by virtue of his closeness to the Creative Nûs needs no guidance, but guides all others. Al-Farâbî identifies him as the inspired man; revelation is the only intermediary between him and the Creative Nûs: in Islamic terminology, he is the Prophet. In spite of the Hellenistic, neo-Platonic garb, al-Farâbî's Ideal City represents the Islamic state; the first cause that stands highest and from which emanates all else, is identical with Allâh.

Below the Principal Leader, and dependent on his guidance,

are sub-leaders who conduct the various affairs of society. Beneath these lesser leaders, guided by and dependent on them, the citizens are ranked according to their innate capacities or their education and training. Each has the obligation, and at the same time, the privilege, to contribute in his own station and according to his own capacity to the affairs of the Ideal State.

The essential factor in this system is its direct relation to the Creative *Nûs* which is the highest emanation of the All-One; therefore, the Ideal State belongs to the All-One; it is, in Islamic terminology, Allâh's state. This *Madînah al-Fâdilah* has not yet been attained in reality, but can only be visualized; it is, in fact, an Utopia.

Ibn Khaldûn and al-Farâbî differ in their interpretation of kingship. The former, observing the actual conditions in his own environment, considers kingship to be natural and necessary for the survival of society in the struggle of all against all. The king rises from among his group; he is the exponent of its "group spirit" *'asabîyah* and is carried by it. Ibn Khaldûn considers that spirit the most potent force in human associations, even in their most primitive forms. But kingship is "based on conquest and coercion" and therefore conflicts with the divine intentions for the world revealed in divine law.

This dichotomy does not exist in al-Farâbî's Ideal State. In the neo-Platonic system, the idea of kingship, too, emanates from the All-One; therefore, the king cannot fall into the pitfalls, which Ibn Khaldûn regards as inevitable, of usurping more power than is his due and of using it for his own ends. In the Ideal State, all authority rests in the king; but he is also responsible for organizing the state in such a way that "the parts dovetail and assist each other in attaining happiness." Interestingly, al-Farâbî's system leaves room for sharing both authority and responsibility. If the high qualities required for the First Leader cannot be found in one person, leadership may be shared by a group of people each of whom represents one or more of the necessary qualities.

In spite of the intimate connexion between the Ideal State and the All-One, its laws are not immutable. For though historical states exist in time and follow each other in its course, they form part of the same will and intention. Therefore, as long as the fundamentals of the Ideal State are not violated, changes in the laws necessitated by changing actual conditions are possible without conflict, for the continuity is safeguarded by these fundamental principles. Progress is in harmony with, if not directed by, tradition.

III.

Neither al-Farâbî nor Ibn Khaldûn had any opportunity to translate his philosophic and sociologic theories into practice. This task confronts modern Muslim nations; it is complicated by the necessity of making their social system and the organs directing it acceptable to their own people, while at the same time they must be able to hold their own before the judgement of the West. The test lies in their concept of the relation between religion and the state, and their attitude towards the minorities in it.

The constitutions of some of the nations professing Islam have been in effect for some decades. That of Iran dates from 1906, the Iraqian from 1924/5, that of Afghanistan from 1931. (The last-mentioned is, in effect, a reiteration and affirmation of the prescripts of Canon Law, except for specifically forbidding slavery.) Other Muslim countries, e.g., Yemen and Sa'ûdî Arabia, are still governed in the medieval manner in total dependence on their ruler. Only Syria, Indonesia and Pakistan were founded after World War II; the Syrian Constitution dates from the year 1950. For this book, the most recent constitutions are the most relevant ones; they are those of Indonesia and Pakistan, and by way of comparison, that of the Egyptian Republic. For in the process of their drafting, the modern problems were most carefully considered.

Indonesia is currently governed in accordance with the "Provisional Constitution of the Republic of Indonesia" dated 1950. Though Islam is the dominant religion in the country, neither that faith, nor the Koran or the *Sunnah* are mentioned in that document. Religious feeling is shown in two contexts. The Preamble acknowledged the nation's existence "thanks to God's blessings and by His mercy" and speaks of "the recognition of the Divine Omnipotence, Humanity, National Consciousness, Democracy and Social Justice." Its article 18 states that "Everyone is entitled to freedom of religion, conscience and thought"; article 43 elaborates on these two statements, but does not specifically refer to Islam. In this way, Indonesia serves notice that she does not consider herself an *Islamic* state, though internally the debate about the predominance of that faith and its influence on public affairs is by no means ended. It may be inferred, too, that article 58 refers to the ethnic, not the religious, association of the Chinese, European and Arab minority groups and their representation in the House of Representatives. Indonesian political theory consequently does not offer much food for thought to the Islamist—or possibly only in the negative.

Pakistan, on the other hand, offers a strong contrast; for a passionate debate on the problems posed by its very origin had preceded her proclamation as an Islamic Democratic Republic and the official adoption of her Constitution. The very severity of the discussion produced the restraint and intellectual superiority of the Constitution, its moderation and legal tenability without violating basic Muslim principles or the rights of any of its citizens.

The Pakistani Constitution contains only one symbolic reservation: the head of the Federation must be a Muslim. Neither the provincial governors, nor any other officer of the state must necessarily profess Islam. Other modern nations in which that religion predominates make the same reservation for the head of their state. The purely symbolic meaning of this stipulation has frequently been emphasized in public statements by leading Pakistanis.

The rights of the minorities are fully guaranteed. In fact, the Constitution speaks only of "citizens"; it refers to "minorities" only to safeguard expressly their human rights and their status as citizens of their nation. Persecution of the *dhimmî*, as shown in a previous chapter, had always been a breach of Canon Law; but is is a new departure for modern Muslim states to incorporate binding provisions as an integral factor into their constitutions. Such guarantees are found in those of Iraq, Syria, and Iran as well. Neither Ibn Khaldûn nor al-Farâbî had made any provisions for the place of the non-conformant in the state they visualized; they were tacitly left outside the pale of their systems, by al-Farâbî as belonging to the "error category," by Ibn Khaldûn by not participating in the "group solidarity" 'asabîyah.

Pakistan's long struggle for a synthesis of the old and the new in her Constitution is not an isolated phenomenon; it is but one of the many aspects of the modernizing and liberalizing trends in contemporary Islam.

For some eighty years Egypt had been governed by the British. But she had gradually been gaining some measure of self-government and, in 1923, been given a constitution though it was of British inspiration and design. This established Islam as the state religion, but guaranteed free exercise of any religion and faith; all Egyptians without distinction of race, tongue and religion were to be equal before the law. The efficacy of this constitution was hampered by Egypt's two-pronged struggle against the British and against her ruling classes that were led by the king. In 1936, the country gained full sovereignty and in 1952, the king was forced to abdicate; in 1953, Egypt was declared a republic and in 1956, a new, government-sponsored constitution came into force. It reiterated the principle of equality of all Egyptians before the law without discrimination on account of race, origin, language, religion or creed; it guaranteed unrestricted freedom of worship. Islam was established as the state religion. As in the Indonesian Constitution, no mention was made of Koran and *Sunnah*, nor was there any demand for laws to be enacted and the affairs to be conducted in conformity with Islamic principles, a provision that had been so dominating an issue in the deliberations of the Pakistani legislators.

As an illustration, it may be of interest to mention that the synagogues in Cairo are still (1957) open and undisturbed. Services are held on every Sabbath and holidays. In 1950/51, a policeman was posted at the entrance to the beautiful Great Synagogue in one of the main streets in the centre of Cairo; in 1955, this precaution had been abandoned even on the New Year and the Day of Atonement. People entered the synagogue with the same unconcern as they do in the United States. On the other hand, in September 1955, the Coptic Church was forced to surrender its jurisdiction over its co-religionists in personal law to the Egyptian courts.

IV.

Though ancient traditional concepts are still alive in the conduct of private as well as public affairs, a slow evolutionary process of change can be detected in religious attitudes. In the decisive decades before the turn of the century, Egypt had had the great advantage of having, in the Azhar, the stronghold of tradition, a religious leader who had grasped the inescapable need for a fresh approach and new answers and solutions to ancient problems. Muhammad 'Abduh, an acknowledged scholar of undoubted orthodoxy, commanded the respect of the doctors of Islam. But he had had a glimpse of the West while living in exile in Paris. Steeped in ancient scholarship, 'Abduh realized that Islam would have to become again pliable as it had been in its golden age. Only then could it halt the spread of irreligiosity amongst its followers who protested against the rigidity of its tradition-bound guardians and defenders. The influence of Muhammad 'Abduh and his disciples can be felt everywhere in Egypt, in the personal attitude towards Islam as well as in its official administration. The Egyptian intellectuals are Believers without bigotry; they keep Islamic laws and rituals and subscribe to its religious tenets, but are open to western influence without losing their faith. In the masses, Islam is practised fervently, lovingly and with devotion, but without fanaticism and hatred of the non-Muslim.

Sheikh 'Abduh's moderation gradually affected Muslim life in Egypt. Sentiment towards century-old habits and traditional

customs changed subtly. Without openly challenging Canon
Law or abolishing its institutions, interpretation was gradually
adapted to that change in outlook and brought into conformance
with new directions of social and religious thought. Disputes
arising out of Muslim family, personal and inheritance law, for
instance, have for some years been brought before special courts,
neither entirely secular nor entirely religious; their decisions
comply increasingly with the spirit of Islam without undue
emphasis on its letter. Civil litigations involving plural marriage have increasingly been decided in a manner favouring
monogamy without ever openly opposing polygamy or declaring
it illegal. But none of the constitutions discussed above mention plural marriage; they neither abolish nor specifically allow
it. The solution will probably be left to evolution.

In pre-Partition India, too, the new spirit made itself felt.
Muhammad Iqbâl publicly and forcefully supported the reforms
in Turkey which had been more radical than any contemplated
then or now in other modern Muslim states. In view of Iqbâl's
influence on Muslim India, his inconsistency when it came to
supporting changes in certain customs of his own environment
is regrettable. But he was probably aware of the limits to which
he could go without antagonizing the reactionary religious
leaders of Indian Islam; yet, Pakistan's moderate, forward-looking Constitution would not have been possible without him.

A study of this constitution reveals unswerving devotion to
the dominant principles of state-craft in our modern age. For
its creators, "democracy," "will of the people," "social justice"
are not empty phrases. As the detailed amplifications within the
document show, they are understood and conceived in their
"modern," western sense, politically their truest since they are
rooted in Roman law. Pakistanis can fully subscribe to them
because they do not clash with fundamental tenets of their
religion; they even implement Islamic principles and practice.
Indeed, references of modern Muslim apologists to the "Electoral
College," the *Shûrà*, in 'Umar ibn al-Khattâb's time, or their
insistence in the basic democracy of Islam, should not simply be
dismissed with condescension as naïve, or as the desire to show

how "progressive" ancient Islam already was; such statements have deeper significance. They express the conviction that modern practices can be accepted without hesitation by an Islamic state and that Muslims detect an affinity with ancient ideas of their faith in modern political practices. What else can "tradition" mean but the continuity between new developments and ancient, time-honoured customs?

Pakistan, Egypt, and other countries have tacitly introduced into their political and legal systems modern ideas and practices in issues where no specific Islamic law or custom existed or where modern thought did not clash with them. This was helped by the gradual emergence of regional legal practice in the courts of the various Muslim countries that had become acceptable to their nationals and that was increasingly looked upon as their *Muslim* law. Its existence helped to develop state law. Only where definite and explicit legislation or decisions were found in Koran and *Sunnah* did the Pakistani legislators find adjustment difficult. Thus, in spite of vigorous pressure, polygamy has not been declared illegal either in the Constitution or in a court of law; *purdah* has not been abolished, nor have *purdah* institutions been prohibited. But women have been given equal political and legal rights, and in public places, other than those "intended for religious purposes only there shall be no discrimination against any citizen on the ground of race, religion, caste, *sex* (the author's italics) or place of birth" (part II, art. 14).

A great deal of anxious discussion, not entirely devoid of animosity, had been devoted to the position of "minorities" in the Islamic State of Pakistan. In the West, the medieval principle of "cuius regio, eius religio" was abolished, through the Peace of Westphalia, as early as 1648; freedom of religion and of conscience, though not civic equality, was thereby established. In consequence, the secular state in the West, that is, in modern times, the majority of existing nations, does, in principle, not require of its citizens to adhere to one particular creed or faith. In the Islamic countries this freedom is in process of evolving.

The height of hostility against an alleged minority within

Pakistan probably was reached in the riots by fanatic Muslim groups in the Punjab against the Ahmadîyah movement. The *Report of the Court of Inquiry* makes extremely interesting reading. It is enlightening for the confusion obtaining in the minds of bigoted and politically misguided, biased groups, but even more so for the sincerity, moderation and progressive, constructive thinking of the Court. The *Report* brings the problem of minorities into sharp relief; its findings are applicable, beyond the specific case before it, to all minorities in the country. It states concisely the traditional theological positions, but shows the ineptness of their orthodox defenders who, simply by undiscerning insistence on Tradition, were enmeshed in their own illogic and contradictions. In contrast, the comments of the Court show their eagerness to maintain the fundamentally sound ideas and the basic principles of Koran and Canon Law; but they apply common sense and constructive interpretation and make the most of the positive factors.

In the modern world, the Muslim not infrequently finds himself a citizen of a non-Muslim country. From the Muslim point of view, the test case for the religious situation of a Muslim in a non-Muslim state and the implied theoretical dilemma is found in India. The problem was put to the "Divines" interrogated in the Inquiry of the Punjab Disturbances. They testified that all Muslims living under non-Muslim sovereignty ought, for religion's sake, to emigrate to a country within the Abode of Islam. One should, however, note the critical comment of the Court of Inquiry on the extreme position of these 'Ulamâ' and their emphasis on the evident impossibility of carrying out that postulate in practice.

In actual fact, the Pakistan Citizenship Act of 1951 had long ago put an end to any legal controversy by defining the term "citizen of Pakistan." Its most important provision, in the framework of this study, is that no special racial, religious or ethnic qualifications are required for holding or acquiring citizenship. The Constitution solemnly proclaims that "all citizens are equal before law and are entitled to equal protection of law." In the definition of the term "citizen," it refers to the

Citizen Act. No disabilities, nor second-rate citizenship, are attached to the "minorities" in the Constitution. When they are mentioned as such, it is to safeguard their rights, not to curtail them, to emphasize their integration, not to exclude them. During the deliberations and the drafting stage, the question of "reserved seats" for the minorities in the National and Provincial Assemblies was hotly debated. The Constitution as enacted refers the decision for or against "joint" or "separate" electorate to the National Assembly, a compromise probably arranged in order not to delay its enactment.

In some Muslim countries, e.g., in Iraq and Iran, minority communities, such as the Jews, have long been represented by their own delegates in proportion to their number. The intense attention given to the discussion of this particular problem, particularly in the United States, is due to two reasons. The equality of every citizen is deeply ingrained in the American consciousness; any deviation from it, as e.g., the poll tax in Southern states, is considered an injustice and an encroachment on this right. Furthermore, the contrast of India, in which discrimination was officially discountenanced, made Pakistan's seemingly contrasting attitude appear out of touch with modern concepts.

ISLAM AND NATIONALISM

I.

In his impartial investigation into the validity and consequences of the Muslim claim for Pakistan (*Pakistan or the Partition of India*), B. R. Ambedkar defines "nationality" as "a social feeling. It is a feeling of a corporate sentiment of oneness which makes those who are charged with it feel that they are kith and kin. This national feeling is . . . at once a feeling of fellowship for one's own kith and kin and an anti-fellowship feeling for those who are not one's own kith and kin." Dr. Ambedkar examines the truth of this statement with regard to the Muslims in pre-Partition India and the conclusions to be drawn from it for their particular position. It may equally be taken as a starting point for an examination of the problem of Muslim unity beyond racial, ethnic, or national groupings.

The Indian Muslims were differentiated amongst themselves, but they had been moulded by common historical heritage into a unit that had substituted the awareness of the traits they shared, especially their religion, for the consciousness of the features that separated them. The diversity of Indian Muslims, as now of Pakistanis, was large, ranging from difference in origin, language and colour to religious distinction, such as Shî'ism and Sunnism. Their unity was enhanced by their feeling distinct from non-Indian Muslims. That is an important factor. For in spite of the spiritual unity of Islam and its concept of brotherhood, its community of faith and ritual, belief in Allâh and His Messenger, the separatist forces in the Muslim world are, as they always were, strong.

The second half of the nineteenth century saw the rise of Pan-Islamism, a movement of strong spiritual and political potential. Its moving spirit, Jamâl ad-Dîn al-Afghânî (1838/9-1897), called on all Muslims, regardless of their ethnic, linguistic or national affiliation, to rally for a spiritual rebirth of Islam and a revival of its political power. His aim was to shake off western domination and to establish spiritual, intellectual and economic independence for the East. A strong consciousness of Islamic values and of its unifying power seemed a good weapon in that fight.

Pan-Islamism failed because of the nationalistic countercurrents within the Muslim countries of the late nineteenth century that were exploited by the western powers for their own aims. They were helped by the intrigues of influential personalities at the Muslim courts against al-Afghânî, as prevalent when Pan-Islamism was at its height as they had been in the medieval Islamic empire.

The immensity and over-expansion of the latter under the Umaiyads and 'Abbasides made its cohesion and the unanimity of all its members difficult to achieve. The variety of ethnic and cultural groups, of languages, races and social customs prevented harmony in outlook, purpose and approach to religious issues. Antagonisms amongst its components outweighed the synergic forces of Islam. Inner weakness combined with attacks of enemies from without to counteract incipient political and spiritual unity. When assembled at the Ka'bah during the pilgrimage, Muslims from all over the world felt as "kith and kin"; but the ceremonies over, this spiritual kinship was all but forgotten. Thus it was from the very beginning of Islam's world expansion, thus it is today. The pilgrims disperse and become again Egyptians, Syrians, Iraqis, Iranians, Pakistanis and Indonesians.

Pan-Islamism was the first attempt in modern times to emphasize the uniting forces in Islam. Unfortunately, the negative factor in it was also strong; it only achieved a rally of the Muslims *against* the West, not *for* creative purposes. This negativism has since been the misfortune of every effort at unification and at channeling the synergic forces in Islam into concerted ideals and actions. Pan-Islamism arose from the emerging consciousness of the antagonism between East and West, resentment against western domination and eastern aspirations to greatness. It was a negative, not a positive impulse and it failed because of its negativism.

The same is true of Pan-Arabism. This movement called only upon the Arab part of the Muslim world and, by dropping Islam as the decisive criterion, appealed to the non-Muslim Arab as well. But again the Arab world hardly ever rallied to any positive effort, such as reforms of the social conditions in their lands. The strongest incentive to co-operative effort was always some external foe, colonialism, imperialism, Britain, France, and the latest comer in the line of enemies, Zionism and the state of Israel, often accused of being an instrument of the former.

The most recent attempt to consolidate the Arab world and give its endeavours concentration and direction was the Arab League. However, it was, from the outset, inherently weak. Though it was not exclusively inspired by foreign political interests, these were utilizing the latent desire for unity and concerted action among the Arabs for their own purposes. But the only sphere in which the Arab League was able to unite all Arabs, once it had shaken off foreign influence, was the fight against Israel, once more a negative effort. When that had failed, at least for the time being, the particularistic aims and interests of its member states counteracted its unifying trends and tendencies. Even attempts at co-ordination of their efforts in the economic and cultural spheres, in spite of some slight success, were overpowered by the stronger centrifugal forces of their political aspirations. The Arab League united the Arabs in their fight against western domination; it was called into play whenever a constellation of power politics threatened some vital interest of all or any of the Arab states. But negative attitudes and impulses are uncreative, even destructive, not least for those who use them. Significantly the Arab League had been declared all but dead by the Arabs themselves in March 1956, when its member states again rallied to an Arab cause in the Suez crisis—once more against a threat from without, not for a constructive purpose within. The recent unification of Egypt and Syria and the federation between Iraq and Jordan of 1958 were also defensive reactions against political pressures. Neither their effect on the movement towards Arab unity, be it favourable or adverse, nor their impact on the development of Islam can as yet be assessed.

The movement of the Muslim Brotherhood (al-Ikhwân al-Muslimûn) combined reactionary religious orthodoxy with chauvinistic nationalism and some demand for social reform. Its emphasis on the religious revival of Islam enabled it to carry its propaganda beyond the frontiers of Egypt, the country of its origin, and it claimed large numbers of supporters in other Arab and Muslim countries. Their insistence on extreme Islamic orthodoxy is alien to the Egyptian mind; it seems to have been a means to achieve their nationalistic aims. In 1947, the author used to listen over the radio to their meetings from which she was excluded as a woman; the tenor of the speeches and sermons, the ever-increasing tension of the audience which frequently interrupted the speaker by shouting Allâhu akbar "Allâh is great," reminded her frighteningly of Hitler mass meetings in Nazi Germany. In 1950, when the movement was proscribed, she discussed its impact with some government employees in an Egyptian provincial town whose guest she was. They admitted membership in the proscribed movement and emphasized its spiritual, national and social aims. They estimated that there were still some three million members in Egypt and some hundred thousand abroad.

II.

Inherent negativism was one reason for the failure of Pan-Islamism and for the comparative ineffectiveness of Pan-Arabism, both in its earlier form and that of the Arab League. The other, not entirely unconnected with the former, was the awareness of basic distinctions that go back into ancient times. Differences between the Muslims of the Indo-Pakistan subcontinent, the Indonesian archipelago, the Iranians and the Arabs are obvious; they are ethnic, racial and linguistic. Far less evident are those among the Arabs themselves. For these, too, were conscious of distinctive heritage.

An ancient animosity between "Qais" and "Mudar," the Arabs of South and North Arabian origin, raged in the early Islamic empire and provoked strife, jealousy and fighting; it was used by political groups in their struggle for power. This has been paralleled in modern times by the rivalry between the Hashimite and the Sa'ûdî dynasties. The ancient provinces were divided, too, by political frictions. Syria was the stronghold of the Umaiyads, Iraq that of the 'Abbasides; the former had their capital in Damascus, the latter mainly in Baghdad. Historically, these dynasties had different alignments and religious tendencies. The Umaiyads were Arabs, conscious and proud of their Arab heritage; their religion sat lightly on them. Many of the 'Abbaside caliphs had non-Arab mothers, Iranians or slave women of various racial origins; they did not possess that close affinity with the Arab element in Islam. With them, religion and its problems carried weight.

From these differences, a logical, or at least, an emotional line leads to the nationalisms and antagonisms in the Arab world of today. Egypt, now aspiring to leadership in it, was amongst the first to assert her individuality and to develop a strong dynasty of her own under the Fatimides (969-1171). From that reign to the present, she repeatedly asserted her claim to leadership within the Muslim domain and fought against the rulers in the eastern parts of the caliphate. Under the Aiyubides (Saladdin and his successors, 1171-1250) and the Mamluks (1250-1516) she extended her domination over Syria and Palestine. In modern times, under Muhammad 'Alî (1769-1849), Egypt was the first to assert her right to independent action, though nominally part of the Ottoman empire. The Khedive waged a successful war against the Turks in Syria and fought the Wahhabis in Arabia, both parts of that empire. Thus Egypt began her development as a modern nation with interests and political aspirations of her own. Even her occupation by the British could not diminish her strong feeling of being a nation apart.

The ancient Egyptian heritage played a decisive role in this self-assertion. It strengthened, as it still does, her national pride as well as her awareness of being distinct from other Arab-speaking people. But Egypt is not alone in possessing a glorious past; Iraq and Syria can lay claim to similar ancient glories. The Syrians are heirs to the Canaanites, and Iraq can point to the ruins of Nineveh and Babylon and to Baghdad, the seat of Harûn ar-Rashîd; it was the intellectual capital of Islam in the east competing through art and science with Cairo, the seat of the Azhar, in the west.

None of these nations, in our time, are racially homogeneous. The Copts of Egypt, of ancient Egyptian stock, live next to descendents of the Arab conquerors or Arab re-migrants into her territory from North West Africa. Many Egyptians proudly boast of their Turkish ancestors who had come to Egypt with Muhammad 'Alî, himself not a Turk but an Albanian. Even descent from Circassian women was several times pointed out to the writer. In Iraq and in Syria, too, non-Arab and non-Semitic races have intermixed with the Arabs.

III.

Repeatedly in the history of Islam, its unifying forces had been in conflict with those that kept its components apart. For decades, at least since World War I, the world has again been witnessing that struggle between the interests common to all Muslims and the demands of national self-interest. Sometimes, these contradictory stimuli are active at the same time. Then a nation may be bound by its national interests to a western power while it sympathizes nonetheless with aspirations of a sister Arab or Muslim nation. At the time of this writing, Iraq and Pakistan are faced with this paradox in the Suez Canal and the Arab-Israel conflicts against their alliance with the West in the so-called Baghdad Pact.

Thus, side by side with the sentiment of Islamic brotherhood, currents other than religious ones led towards consolidation of segments within the Muslim world. The process of secular unification, in evidence in our time, is repeating, possibly with greater intensity, historical trends already prevailing at the time when the Islamic empire was at its zenith, often based on geographic and socio-economic conditions. Medieval Europe underwent a comparable process. From within the Holy Roman Empire emerged the particularistic interests that consolidated into the great European nations, France, Germany, Italy, etc., and the nationalisms that characterized European history well into the twentieth century.

In our generation, the East and the Arab world are passing through the phase of youthful assertion of their national independence typical in the development of nations. The West is just maturing into the stage in which particularistic and chauvinistic aims are being submerged into international co-operation and mutual toleration—so-to-speak, "the United Nations mentality." Even the West itself is still groping towards full maturity, and selfish interests frequently break through to determine its actions. But the western nations have learned by bitter experience that chauvinism is doomed by the very fact that it might clash with other chauvinisms.

The East is just entering the phase of extreme nationalism.

President Sukarno of Indonesia expressed it in his address to the Congress in Washington in 1956. He could rightly claim to speak for all of Asia, not alone for his own country, when he contrasted Asian and African nationalism as "a young and pro-gressive creed" with the West's concept of nationalism as "an out-of-date doctrine."

Many conflicting tendencies are involved in this develop-ment. The new nations of the Near and Middle East are pre-dominantly Muslim. Nonetheless, their political interests, some-times their very survival, demand political alignments that counteract the centripetal forces of Islam. Thus, Turkey, Iraq, Iran and Pakistan are joined with the West, for fear of powers that threaten their existence as sovereign states. This alliance with the West is resented by other Islamic nations. At the same time, other interests bind Near and Middle East countries to South East Asia, in the Bandung and Colombo and SEATO groups. This phenomenon proves that neither Arabism nor Islam are any longer the decisive or exclusive justification for political alliances. Even within these international groups, politi-cal considerations have at least the same potency as common racial and religious ties.

Within the individual nations themselves, the same trend can be discerned. In spite of the diversity of races and religions in the Near and Middle Eastern states, national identifications are supplanting the former religious, ethnic or linguistic ones. Not so long ago, any Near or Middle East man would have identified himself by his religious or tribal affiliation or his geographical provenance. Now in spite of the variety of religious denominations, Muslim as well as non-Muslim, in Egypt, Syria, Lebanon, Iraq, Iran, a national consciousness is arising. That is also true of Pakistan, in spite of the often expressed fear that the insistence in her religious foundations would prevent national integration of non-Muslims. The solemn proclamation of Egypt, in her Constitution of 1956, as an Arab nation—an expression also used in the constitutions of other Arab states—seems to be based on opportunist political motives. In 1950/51, many ordinary Egyptians were opposed to the involvement of their country in the affairs of the Arabs. "Let those Arabs fight their own wars, we are Egyptians," the author then heard repeatedly in discussions on the Arab-Israel conflict. In 1955, that outlook had changed through later political developments.

In the Palestine issue these conflicting emotions and attitudes are put to the test. By associating Jerusalem with the Prophet, it became for the Muslims *al-Quds* "The Holy City," as sacred to them as it is to the Jews and the Christians. Islamic legend interpreted a Koranic vision as a miracle that had happened to the Prophet. "Celebrated be the praises of Him who took His servant a journey by night from the Sacred Mosque to the Remote Mosque, the precincts of which We have blessed, to show him of Our signs!" (Sûrah 17, verse 1). This verse mentions neither Mecca nor Jerusalem by name, yet it was held to describe a miraculous night journey by the Prophet from Mecca to Jerusalem, his ascension thence to "the highest heaven" and his return to Mecca before dawn.

Since the surrender of Jerusalem to the Arabs thirteen centuries ago, Palestine had been both "Abode of Islam" and Arab territory. From the Arab point of view, the partition of the country in 1948 and the establishment of the state of Israel therefore represented a twofold provocation. It deprived Arabs of a land that had been theirs for many generations, and it converted part of the "Abode of Islam" into "Abode of War." In theory, as explained before, this called for *Jihâd* to restore it to the sovereignty of Islam. That duty devolved upon every Muslim, regardless of nationality or race. To some extent the whole Muslim world responded to it, though most Islamic nations supported the Arab cause merely by political, not military, action.

In addition, the resistance to the state of Israel is directed against its western orientation. Israel emphasizes its political and technological, as well as its cultural and intellectual bonds with the West. The Arabs, too, are eager to open their countries to western technology; but, in common with most Asian nations, they have grown somewhat wary of too far-reaching western influence. Rightly or wrongly they began to regard Zionism, and later Israel, as an outpost of that "imperialism" and "colonialism" that they were fighting. Unfortunately, Israel's attack on Egypt in the autumn of 1956 could not but serve to strengthen this belief and, in consequence, to intensify Arab hostility towards Israel.

IV.

Thus, in the struggle between those two strong forces, nationalism and religion, the former at present has emerged victorious. Religion is still a vital factor, but in a contest between national and religious impulses, the latter prevail only if they either parallel the national interests or, at least, do not hamper them. Turkey after her revolution severed the conduct of her affairs consciously and rigourously from religious considerations; she is still the only Muslim nation to have done so. Ever since, she did not allow any religious sentiments of her citizens to influence her actions as a nation, nor the surviving religious bodies to exert pressure on her political life. After years of such suppression, she was able, in 1953, to relax her strict prohibition of official religious instruction and has even introduced state-controlled theological training schools (to which, by the way, women, too, are admitted). In Indonesia, in spite of her avowed organization as a secular state, Muslim groups are still powerful and exert strong political pressure; they are a force to be reckoned with internally. But in her foreign affairs, she is a secular nation consistently pursuing her own interests regardless of religious considerations.

Egypt, too, in spite of calling herself "an integral part of the Arab Nation," is chauvinistically Egyptian. In fact, a definition of what constitutes "The Arab Nation" needs to be given; an "Arab Nation" does not exist either legally or in practice. There is the "Arab League"; but that is a loose organization of sovereign states that are in no way bound to act according to the decisions of its council. In fact, the only issue in which the League of Arab States can expect its member states to act unanimously with a high degree of confidence, is the Arab-Israel conflict. But the term "Arab Nation" is vague and merely the expression of a sentiment; it is somewhat reminiscent of Nazi

Germany's "blood and soil" doctrine. A. A. Hourani, himself
an Arab, has analysed the idea and the sentiments on which
"Arabism" and "the feeling of Arab Unity" are based; his able
and illuminating analysis serves to emphasize that "an Arab
Nation" does not exist except, possibly, as an ideal and a somewhat eschatological dream. There are *Arab nations* and these
will act as Arabs when that action will not interfere with their
interests as independent states. Yet, in 1958, Lebanon, a member of the Arab League, felt impelled to appeal to the United
Nations in a dispute with other Arab states.

To what extent Islam will remain the decisive factor in
Pakistan cannot be fully assessed yet, since the issues are still
in flux in that nation, and public sentiment is just beginning
to crystallize. She will give moral support to other Muslim
nations, e.g., to the Arabs in their struggle in North West
Africa or in the Palestine issue. Though supporting them at the
United Nations vigourously, she is consistently following her own
political line and reasoning, without ever losing sight of her
own interests. Significantly, after the comparatively short time
of her existence as a nation, national consciousness is replacing
the emphasis on the religious aspects of her unity. Pakistanis
are beginning to stress their national rather than their religious
affiliation. In conversation with the author, Pakistani Christians pointed to the evolving consolidation of the country and
the integration of her Christian and other non-Muslim citizens
into her body politic. The coming generation, they predicted,
unencumbered with the cruel memories of the past and of Partition, would grow up as Pakistanis by nationality and Muslims
or Christians or Hindus by religion. To her regret, the writer
had no opportunity to discuss this question with Pakistani Hindus, for her stay was limited to West Pakistan.

The fear expressed by Muslims whom she met in India
that Pakistan would become, "like the Near East, disorganized
and politically reckless," seemed to stem from their apprehension
for their own future; such statements were made mainly in
discussing unsolved problems between India and her neighbour,
such as the Kashmir issue. On the other hand, Indian Muslims

and their leaders are trying strenuously to become integrated emotionally as well as politically into India, and to identify themselves nationalistically with it, however deeply they may profess Islam. Between the Indian and the Pakistani Muslims a feeling of both attraction and rejection seems to exist. Until so very recently they had been united in their religion as well as in their political allegiance; as Muslims, the two groups feel a close affinity with each other. As Indian or Pakistani nationals, however, they are divided in matters of principle. The Pakistani seems to reproach the Indian Muslim for not joining the Islamic state; psychological factors cause that resentment. The Pakistani feels that the Indian Muslim chose the easy way out and did not undergo the same hardships, loss of fortune, of life, and, last not least, of a beloved home; he was not forced to build up a new life. The Indian Muslim rejects the creation of a "religious" state and is opposed to "making religion the basis of a nation"—possibly sometimes a rationalization for less exalted reasons for his decision. He asserts that he fought with Gandhi for Independence, not with Jinnah for Partition. The Pakistani is homesick, but he is slowly building a new home; he will possibly become the more deeply attached to it for having created it himself for his children and his children's children. They will be secure. Though the Indian Muslim firmly asserts his integration into the secular state of India, he cannot yet feel completely sure for generations to come. He realizes that the future depends on circumstances, personalities and unpredictable emotions.

Paradoxically, the Muslim community has emerged strengthened from this tug of war between conflicting tendencies among its members and within the nations of which it is composed. It has clarified the issues in the Muslims' own minds and has brought into focus the differences as well as the similarities. They share the creative, positive forces in their national aspirations, the spiritual force of Islam and the resurrection of their vitality as peoples. It is unfortunate that this should so often be used for chauvinistic aims, for aspirations after political power and aggressiveness directed especially against the West. President Sukarno's address to the Congress should be heeded in both East and West: "For us of Asia and Africa, nationalism is a young and progressive creed. We do not equate nationalism with chauvinism, and we do not interpret nationalism as meaning the superiority of our peoples over others. No! For us, nationalism means the rebuilding of our nations; it means the effort to provide equal esteem for our peoples; it means the determination to take the future into our own hands. For us, nationalism is the love of country and the determination to improve it. . . . Nationalism may be an out-of-date doctrine for many in this world; for us of Asia and Africa, it is the mainspring of our efforts." Sukarno might, and ought to, have added that it is also a struggle for regaining the ancient spiritual values and applying them to the reconstruction of society, whatever its religion. It is a tragic inheritance from the wrongs wrought in past centuries that these basically valid and high aims are so frequently distorted and the enthusiasm of the people directed towards debased objectives. Even Sukarno turned, immediately after these intrinsically valid phrases, to political demands and accusations, too often heard and no longer justified, against western imperialism and colonialism.

For its own sake, as well as for the sake of world peace, the West would wish that Muslim nationalism might mature quickly and outgrow its present self-concentration; ancient Islamic internationalism shows the way. And if the Muslim would want a fellow Muslim to lead him in this quest, let him turn to Muhammad Iqbâl who almost thirty years ago has found the path through Islam: "For the present, every Muslim nation must sink into her own deeper self, temporarily focus her vision on herself alone, until all are strong and powerful to form a living family of republics. A true and living unity, according to the nationalist thinkers, is not so easy as to be achieved by a merely symbolical overlordship [sc. the caliph and the caliphate]. It is truly manifested in a multiplicity of free independent units whose racial rivalries are adjusted and harmonized by the unifying bond of a common spiritual aspiration. It seems to me that God is slowly bringing home to us that Islam is neither Nationalism nor Imperialism but a League of Nations which recognizes artificial boundaries and racial distinctions for facility of reference only, and not for restricting the social horizons of its members." A road, not too difficult to travel, leads East and West from this concept to the United Nations and One World.

CHAPTER NINE

Modern Thought in Islam

I.

When we look back over the nearly fourteen centuries of Islamic development from its origin in Mecca to the present, the increase in the number of adherents appears staggering. But its spiritual and intellectual growth is equally overwhelming. From a simple, single-minded call to worship, expressed in one sentence, it grew into a complex system of thought, doctrines and laws. Yet, the complexity of twentieth-century Islam is still encompassed in the same one-sentence formula: "There is no god but Allâh; Muhammad is Allâh's Messenger." The spiritual and philosophic thought processes and struggles that were traced in the preceding chapters of this essay, led from the Prophet's own call to Islam to the fervent, deeply sincere affirmation of this truth by the modern sophisticated Muslim.

Religious and spiritual conflicts, however, are never solved once and for all in spite of dogmas and the vigilance of the clergy over their observance. They are so personal and individual that no pronouncement *ex cathedra* will spare a sensitive mind the obligation to seek for new solutions as if these problems had never been solved before. Men in each new generation in Islam capable of creative thought were therefore impelled to feel, to use a Jewish simile, as if they themselves were standing at the foot of Mount Sinai waiting to receive the Torah from the Lord. The stagnation and retrogression of Islam for many centuries was the result of the theologians' refusal to acknowledge this obligation. Their fear that it might destroy Islam deprived it of its vitality; their compulsive submission to precedence robbed it of creativity.

Islam was roused out of this lethargy by the challenge of forces that attacked its spiritual life as they were subjugating the physical environment of its followers. By the revolt of its adherents against the foreign usurpers and their alien laws to whom they had succumbed, Islam began to recover its political and spiritual strength. Indeed, recovery in spirit was a consequence of the political re-awakening. It is almost impossible to separate the two aspects of that regeneration; both were conceived and promoted by the same personalities and were aimed at the same goal.

The spiritual recovery of Islam would have been, if not impossible, at least retarded, without the re-assertion of its political strength; yet, the latter would have been but another colonial uprising that could have been quelled by military power had it not possessed this inherent spiritual force. The twentieth century could not but respond to it, much as the residue of nineteenth-century power-politics may have wished to retard the inevitable process. Politically, colonialism is still fighting against anti-colonialism and nationalism; but spiritually, the western world had to change its outlook and to acknowledge the validity of spiritualities different from its own. The superficial observer may only see the political revolt and its consequences that are often not too pleasant for the West nor entirely beneficial for the East. But the unbiased scholar must view the external manifestations in their historical perspective and recognize their spiritual core.

In the light of the strain and stresses of our present generation, it is essential to comprehend the close interrelation between the political and religious impulses in the awakening of the Muslim East. The emphasis on the religious revival, simultaneous with the use of western knowledge and techniques as an expedient in the fight for independence, shows the indivisibility of Muslim thought. Muslim scholarship had never been departmentalized. Except for the ascetic and the Sûfî, the Muslim scholar did not bury himself in the ivory tower of his scholarly pursuits; he stood in the centre of activities, was courtier and minister of state, spiritual leader and scientist all in one. The line leads from the vizier Nizâm al-Mulk—who founded the great Nizâmîyah University in Baghdad, in the middle of the eleventh century—and Ibn Khaldûn to al-Afghânî, Muhammad 'Abduh, Muhammad Iqbâl and Taha Husain in the last two generations and our own.

Before the East was able to redeem itself from its own spiritual retardation as well as from western domination, it had to acquire the tools for the struggle through western learning. Thus it began, though only partly conscious of it, its Westernization. Egypt was the leader in this process. Muhammad 'Alî, the creator of modern Egypt, realized that he needed an army trained in western skills and modern weapons for the consolidation and expansion of his powers and for the resistance against the threat from the West. This training could only be found in the West. The Khedive therefore sent his officers to European countries, especially to Italy and France, to study military science, mathematics and medicine. He further needed books on these and other subjects and had the works of western scholars translated into Arabic. In addition, he opened schools for the training of his officers in Egypt and made education available to wider circles. Egypt's leadership of the Arab world in the intellectual field had started.

The spiritual and intellectual renaissance of the Muslim world may be regarded as a reaction against its Westernization; but the latter itself had its beginning in the attempt of Islam to re-examine its own foundations in order to rehabilitate itself. Paradoxically, the movement that eventually led to "modernism" was initially inspired by the desire to purify Islam of the innovations that had accrued to it in the course of centuries, not, to rid Islam of its ancient patterns in order to conform with progress. The retrogressive negativism of Wahhabism (best known from Sa'ûdî Arabia, with its emphasis on ancient traditional forms of life, its prohibition of tobacco and silk, and its hostility to the worship of saints) led its opponents to a renewed examination of "innovations," accepted long ago, concerning their positive values for Islam.

This investigation brought about the reform movement that acknowledged the necessity for reorientation of custom and behaviour according to the demands of contemporary life. But no reformer dreamt of denying eternal validity to the basic doctrines of Islam. Reform itself was conscious of the necessity of tradition; it only demanded adjustment of outmoded customs—which at one time themselves had to be accepted into the Islamic pattern by "Consensus"—to new conditions and changing concepts. None of the leading reformers would have denied the truth of the Confession of Faith nor allowed the bases of Islam, the Koran and *Sunnah,* to be invalidated. They reinvestigated solely the validity and justification for modern times of decisions made by the religious authorities a thousand years and more ago.

One field, in particular, needed deeper search for justification lest its acceptance lead to heresy. The concepts of modern science, physics, medicine, geography and astronomy, differed from those of the Middle Ages that had become part of Muslim dogma. They had to be made palatable to the tradition-bound *sheikh* and the Muslim community; for that end, they had to be brought into harmony with holy Scripture. The Koran itself had to lend its authority to uphold them. That was the task that Muhammad 'Abduh had set himself; and thirty years after his death, Muhammad Iqbâl whose knowledge of western mathematics, physics and philosophy far exceeded that of the Sheikh, was trying to resolve the conflict between Scripture and Science. In the atomic age of the mid-twentieth century, the same problem is still occupying the minds of the Muslim thinkers.

II.

The leading exponents of that re-examination have already been mentioned several times in the present essay. They were concerned with three kinds of problems—those of politics, of philosophy and of science. The basic direction of Islam made it inevitable that all of these would involve the religious issue.

These men investigated them from different view points, but eventually came to the same affirmation of the irrefutability of their religion. Nor did the quest conducted in the medium of literature lead to any intrinsically different conclusions. Education, too, had to wrangle with the same problems in their application to the rearing of future generations.

Thus the names of al-Afghânî and Muhammad 'Abduh, of Iqbâl, Taha Husain and Sir Saiyid Ahmad of Aligarh stand for various facets of the modernist movement; they represent the political and religious thinker, the modern philosopher and poet, the literary critic and educator. All were reformers, liberals and progressives; but only Taha Husain could, at least during one period of his creative life, be accused of being a religious dissenter. They shared the personal experience of western culture and its influence on their intellectual development and attitudes. In the present generation, no one has as yet risen to challenge their pre-eminence. The writers, thinkers and men of action in our time are their disciples; their programs derive from them, they expand and enlarge on their thought, but have as yet not created any new ideas.

Each of these masters had been reared in the traditional pattern of Islam, from the study of the Koran in the old-fashioned manner, which Taha Husain described so delightfully in his autobiographical sketch al-Ayâm, to the pursuit of knowledge at the Azhar or other religious centres. In different spheres, through continuing their education in western universities or through other direct contacts with western civilization, they had risen above the intellectual level of their contemporaries who were satisfied with restating traditional attitudes. Thus they became the leaders on the road towards spiritual regeneration and re-creation of the political power of Islam.

Al-Afghânî was the awakener; he was the first to formulate the rising resentment of the East against western political domination and to call for concerted action by all the Muslim peoples against it. He realized that the reassertion of political independence and the spiritual re-awakening of Islam had to go hand in hand; he tried to unite "all" Islamic nations in the

Pan-Islamic movement that he had created. In reality, his call reached mainly those countries that had for many centuries been united in the Muslim, and its successor, the Ottoman empires. The movement touched the Indian Muslims only in so far as it could be applied to their own problems, and al-Afghânî does not seem to have considered Muslims farther east at all. The Indonesians, for instance, who are playing an important role in world affairs in modern times, do not seem to have heeded his call, at the time.

Some reasons for the apparent failure of Pan-Islamism have already been discussed in the preceding chapter. However, the full measure of its impact has become apparent only within the last few decades, though today a Pan-Islamic movement in its original form does not exist. It was the first impulse towards self-assertion rising from within the Muslim community after its many years of dormancy, the ferment that gave direction to latent dreams of a renewal of Islam and a revival of its spiritual and physical strength. The extent of its success can only now be assessed. In al-Afghânî's time, western military might was at its height; the conscience of the world had not yet been roused. Two world wars and the spiritual leadership of great minds in East and West—foremost among them Mahatma Gandhi, Woodrow Wilson, Franklin Delano Roosevelt—were needed to achieve that. In our day, the voice of the East counts in the councils of the world; it can no longer be ignored, nor can those nations any longer be coerced either in the political or in the spiritual and intellectual sphere.

But the Muslims needed more than political renaissance. The religious message of Islam needed affirmation against the onslaught of modern scepticism in the wake of modern science. Al-Afghânî's call for spiritual revival of Islam was taken up by Muhammad 'Abduh—a proof, in modern times, for the intricate interrelation of the political and the religious aspects in Islam. 'Abduh had been al-Afghânî's close collaborator during their exile in Paris. Together they published the famous journal *Al-'Urwah al-Wuthqà* "The Firm Link," the mouth-piece of al-Afghânî's call to unity, the name of which was, character-

istically, taken from a Koranic verse. Searching for the reasons
of the spreading unbelief especially among Muslim youth,
Sheikh 'Abduh realized that that faith needed reorientation in
the light of the new scientific discoveries lest the "firm link"
between the Muslim and his faith be severed. Science, 'Abduh
thought, did not contradict, but rather could serve to affirm,
the eternal truths revealed by Allâh in the Koran; if rightly
understood, they supported each other and served as proof for
one another.

In his commentary on the Koran he tried to harmonize
the new scientific discoveries of the modern age with the concepts of natural phenomena revealed in the holy Book. 'Abduh's
aim was to prove that modern science confirmed the truth of
the latter; the new discoveries in the world of science were only
modern, more specific affirmations of ancient insights. While
modern science proved them by experiment and mathematical
formulas, the Prophet had received them by revelation from
omniscient God and passed them on to mankind in exalted
"prophetic" visionary language. Revealed cosmogony, if ration-
ally explained, and natural science supported each other; the
discoveries of the nineteenth century sustained the Koranic concepts of nature, while the Koran provided proof for modern
science. To do justice to the Azhar Sheikh, it must be admitted that he and his disciples were not alone in this attitude.
Jewish orthodox rabbis and Christian fundamentalists used
exactly the same argument to uphold their belief in the fundamental truth of Scripture in the face of scientific research.
Modern scientific discoveries, thus they claim, far from shattering
the Biblical theories, support them, if only understood correctly,
just as archaeology and assyriology affirm the historical truth
of Biblical events.

If, as was maintained in the "Prologue" to this essay, such
apologetics have an almost tragic aspect—tragic, because they
seem to be futile as an attempt to save sacred doctrine from
the assault of rationalism—they yet stirred 'Abduh's generation
to greater intellectual freedom and to taking up western studies.
A good example of the resulting moderate traditionalism that

was open to "rational" interpretation of the Koran in the light of modern science, is Muhammad Husain Heikal's *Life of Muhammad*. The author was a leading writer, with a distinguished record in Egyptian education (including having been Minister of Education) and in national and international politics; his literary work, too, has greatly stimulated Arab literature. In that biography of the Prophet, he tried to apply the results of modern psychology to the phenomena of prophetic vision, e.g., he attempted to rationalize the miracles related in the Koran, such as the Prophet's miraculous journey, in one night, from Mecca to Jerusalem and back to Mecca. But in the preface to the second and later editions of the work, the author takes the western Islamists to task for their scepticism and repudiates their critical attitude, referring mainly to nineteenth-century studies. Unfortunately, the writer's activities as a leading educator and, later, as the President of the Egyptian Senate and other high political offices, prevented him from following more recent western research. He was therefore unfamiliar with the works of modern scholars, such as F. Buhl, T. Andrae and J. Horovitz, who analysed Muhammad's personality and his conviction of being the carrier of a divine message with understanding and sympathy and gave full credit to his religious sincerity.

Muhammad 'Abduh was not merely concerned with upholding the truth of revelation against modern scepticism. He was also deeply convinced that Islam, if it was to have a future, must reconsider its stand on many of its practical problems and re-formulate the old solutions that were no longer in line with the new ideological, philosophic and social approaches. Thus he became one of the foremost advocates for the re-opening of the "door to free investigation" (*ijtihâd*), the pivot for reform in Islam. To the conservative *sheikhs* and *'ulamâ'* this might sound like rank heresy; but, argued 'Abduh, it meant only a revival of an ancient Islamic institution. He did not demand repudiation of fundamentals of Islam; he merely asked for a fresh examination of the true meaning of Koran and *Sunnah*. In the chapter on "Social Problems," his interpretation of the Koranic texts on marriage and his *Fetwà* on taking interest have already been discussed. They seemed revolutionary at that time; but his statement that Allâh preferred monogamy to polygamy has become the foundation for the changing attitude towards the latter and the intense fight against it in the whole Muslim world. In consequence of Sheikh 'Abduh's decision, interest taking and modern banking methods have become generally accepted practice throughout, though they have lately been challenged by the orthodox parties in Pakistan and are to be deliberated in her parliament.

'Abduh's activities in the educational field had equally far-reaching results. Though his advice bore fruit only after his death, reforms in the general educational system of Egypt as well as changes in the curriculum of the Azhar are ultimately due to him. Religious and political thinkers reached essentially the same conclusion: without western-style education, no revival either in the religious or in the secular sphere would be possible.

To enter 'Abduh's study in the Azhar, preserved exactly as it had been during his life, was a deeply moving experience for the writer. His name had been familiar to her ever since she began her study of Islam at a western university. The Jewish student of Islamic culture and her Muslim companions, one an Azhar *sheikh,* the other its graduate and an Egyptian educator, were standing at his desk, touching the books that he had studied. She spoke to them of her teacher, Josef Horovitz, the son of a well-known rabbi who had been Sheikh 'Abduh's friend. Many times the professor had spoken to his students of the Sheikh's work and ideas: "Sheikh 'Abduh was the most outstanding mind that has risen in Islam after many generations. He stirred the minds of the Muslims in our time and gave new meaning to ancient forms. Like al-Ghazâlî, his mentor, he fought against mechanical following of traditional usage. Like the medieval philosopher, he asked his disciples to realize that God is re-found and His Word understood in every person's mind and heart."

Not very far away from the Azhar Mosque was the ancient

home of the Jewish philosopher Maimonides (1135-1204), the
friend and physician of Saladdin and his son al-Fadl, a place
sacred to a Jew, but historically meaningful also for Egyptians.
Both rooms still seemed to hold the spirit of the men who had
tried to interpret God's Word for their contemporaries. Generation after generation of Jews had studied Maimonides' works;
'Abduh's commentary on the Koran has become the guide for
his disciples and their followers. An unforgettable morning
that found the Jewish visitor and her Muslim friends remember-
ing the friendship between a Muslim *sheikh* and a Jewish
Islamist, and talking of the Jewish philosopher who guided his
people out of perplexities to knowledge, writing in the Arabic
language! The gathering storm in the summer of 1947 between
the Arabs and the Jews of Palestine enhanced the meaning of
this hour.

III.

Twenty years after Sheikh 'Abduh's death, in India, too,
the conflict between revelation and science was again brought
to the fore. Muhammad Iqbâl's studies in western philosophy,
mathematics and physics led him to an inquiry into the foundations of Islamic concepts. His philosophic ideas and his stand
on dogmatic issues were presented in detail in a preceding
chapter and need not be repeated here. The period of his
creative activity coincided with the decisive re-orientation in
western science and the new concept of the universe inaugurated
by Einstein and other great physicists in the first decades of
our century. Being better trained in these disciplines, Iqbâl's
understanding was more penetrating than that of the Azhar
Sheikh, and his application to the religious problems shows
greater insight.

Though he retained the conviction that scientific knowledge alone is not sufficient but has to be supplemented by
spiritual experience, Iqbâl acknowledged the "infinite advance
[that] has taken place in the domain of human thought and
experience since the Middle Ages." In particular, "the theory
of Einstein has brought a new vision of the universe" that may
help to solve the problems common to both religion and phi-

losophy. After reviewing the theories of space and time held by various philosophers or scientists throughout the centuries, he turned to that of Einstein "who," to quote a recent Muslim analysis of Iqbâl's thought, "has revolutionized the whole conception of time and space from the scientific point of view, and has dealt a death-blow both to the determinism of Newton and to the materialism of the 19th century." In the course of his analysis, Iqbâl interpreted Koranic utterances in terms of the modern theories of physics; at the same time, he used them to support their findings. However, summing up his search for the solution of his problems by science, he comes to the conclusion that "we must not forget that what is called science is not a single systematic view of Reality. It is a mass of sectional views of Reality—fragments of a total experience which do not seem to fit together. Natural science deals with matter, with life, and with mind; but the moment you ask the question how matter, life, and mind are mutually related, you begin to see the sectional character of the various sciences that deal with them and the inability of these sciences, taken singly, to furnish a complete answer to your question" (p. 41f.). The writer, not being a scientist or physicist, cannot give an adequate résumé of Iqbâl's line of thought on this problem and would refer those who wish to get acquainted with it to the essay "'Iqbâl's Conception of Time and Space" written by Dr. M. Raziuddin Siddiqi, the Pakistani nuclear physicist and educator.

Iqbâl did not wish to limit his appeal to the confines of Indian Islam. Much of his work was therefore written in Persian instead of Urdu, its vernacular language. His *Lectures* written in English were addressed to the non-Muslim world as well, which 'Abduh who wrote exclusively in Arabic could not reach, except for a few specialists. Urdu and Persian poetry, however, formed the Indian scholar's main vehicle of expression.

Iqbâl's influence in India, as now in Pakistan, was immense, through the progressive, though also in the retarding, elements of his thought. But on balance, the impact of the former should be found more decisive. He shared certain reactionary tendencies with the average minds in his environment; but his forward-looking ideas inspired the intellectual leaders who were searching for an enduring vitality of their religion in the face of conflicts. For all that, Iqbâl was not a revolutionary; by stressing the evolutionary tendency of Islam, inherent in Allâh's own Word, he assured, and still assures, a harmonious growth for Islam in Pakistan, undisturbed by spiritual upheavals. Due to his calm leadership towards a gradual development, the present generation of intellectual leaders who had been his disciples in their student days can be, at once, true Believers and true Progressives. In much of their writings, their struggle for harmonizing this seeming contradiction is still apparent. But, the more Iqbâl's ideas will be studied by western-trained minds, the more effective will be both his caution and his propelling impact.

The most widely known among Egyptian intellectual leaders, Taha Husain, could not have reached his eminence without 'Abduh. For several decades, the Sheikh's thought had been penetrating into the cultural atmosphere of his country and thus had created the intellectual climate in which Taha Husain grew up. Thus, the boy could outgrow the tradition-bound environment into which he had been born, the Egyptian countryside, the village school that taught the Koran and little else, and the venerable Azhar. After studying at the Sorbonne, he became one of the earliest faculty members and later Dean of the Faculty of Humanities at the secular Fu'âd I University in Cairo. As university teacher, Minister of Education and writer, he was the most influential leader of his generation in Egypt towards westernized modern thought.

The distinguishing feature between him and 'Abduh, Iqbâl and other progressive thinkers was the phase—if, indeed, it was only that—of severe criticism of the traditional beliefs. In this, he dared to go farther than any of the modern thinkers and had to endure severe strictures from the orthodox parties. He was forced to retreat somewhat from his extreme position. By asserting that pre-Islamic poetry was in fact the product of much later times, an opinion not shared even by western Orientalists, he also hurt Arab national pride. It is, however, characteristic for the change in Egyptian intellectual outlook that, in spite of that aura of unorthodoxy still clinging to him, Taha Husain became the revered leader of the Egyptian intelligentsia. For the uneducated masses, he was the beloved redeemer who held out the promise of assuaging their intellectual starvation. Against this strong wave of love and devotion, the opposition of the orthodox was of no avail. The political revolution of 1952 deprived him of his office as Minister of Education, but the new leaders did not turn against him personally or deprecate his achievements.

In contrast to Iqbâl and 'Abduh, Taha Husain's main problem was not the reconciliation between science and revelation; nor did he array Islamic against western thought. On the contrary, Taha Husain maintained that their common roots, the Judaeo-Christian and the Greek heritage, make Islam and the West spiritually, intellectually and religiously more compatible than are Islam and the East, that is, India or Japan, the ever-growing political leaning toward them notwithstanding. Taha Husain regretted that trend, at least in its intellectual and spiritual aspects, though the political events of recent years may have made him amenable to a political rapprochement with Asia. Thus, for Taha Husain, Westernization was not a problem, but a necessity, if not a natural outcome of innate qualities.

In a review of Egypt's intellectual progress, Taha Husain must be rated amongst the most influential contemporary personalities. In his essays, which are written in a somewhat archaic, beautiful Arabic style, his progressive thought is consistently expressed, without concessions to retarding traditionalism, in spite of his appreciation of the inherent values of Islam. Through his educational work, he was in a position to make his ideas effective in practice. As Dean of the Faculty, he brought a generation of students under his influence, many of whom became his collaborators in the Ministry of Education (1950-52); others disseminated his ideas as teachers in the schools, colleges and universities of the country.

This interaction between political, philosophic and educational leadership is significant; often, and almost in every Muslim country, they were combined in one person. This is only partly due to a lack of schooled and trained personnel. It is the outcome of the absence of compartmentalization in Islam from which the West suffers. Sheikh 'Abduh, Muhammad Husain Heikal, and Taha Husain in Egypt, Muhammad Iqbâl and Sir Saiyid Ahmad Khan in India, were active in all three fields. The latter, by founding the Anglo-Muslim College in Aligarh, was instrumental in producing several generations of leaders in Indian and Pakistani Islam.

Iqbâl, too, held political office as a member of the Punjab Legislative Assembly; he participated in the Round Table Conference in London 1930-32. These activities offered him a forum in which to assess his philosophy of Islam against the political actualities in the India of his day. Inevitably his reflections on the situation of the Muslim community in that subcontinent led him to the demand for a Muslim state; he was the first person of rank and influence to have publicly formulated as such the latent trend from "communalism" in India towards separate and integrated states. He thus deserved the honour bestowed upon him by his disciples to be acclaimed as the Creator of Pakistan.

Al-Afghânî and 'Abduh, both religious thinkers as well as active political reformers, paved the way for Sa'd Zaghlûl (died 1927), the hero of Egyptian independence. Muhammad 'Alî Jinnah, Pakistan's Qa'id-i-A'zam "Great Leader," had, in the decade of germination, Iqbâl's active support for the idea of Pakistan.

It is striking that literary works played a far less significant role in the discussion of the weighty intellectual issues. Many political essays were published, but most dealt with the struggle for national independence, or with the social problems of Muslim countries; some study was devoted to questions of philosophy and aesthetics. The religious conflicts were hardly ever treated in a literary fashion. The search for such treatment will lead again to Heikal who in his earliest work, a novel called Zaynab, published first anonymously, broached the subject of women's emancipation. Many writers dealt with the problem

of tradition or reform in Islam; but a novel of first rank subli-
mating the conflicts involved into the realm of art is still to
come.

Nor does there exist any literature that would appeal to
the whole world of Islam outside the religious field; it would
have to be written in a language understood by all, at that. Already in medieval times national literatures developed alongside
the religious works or those on Tradition and Canon Law. The
Shah Nameh, for instance, the Iranian national epos, was composed in the tenth century, to keep the Iranian national spirit
alive; in Spain, poetry developed that did not conform to the
classic Arab-Islamic style. But though Arabic is still the sacred
tongue of all Muslims, it is no longer used nor even understood
by all Islamic peoples. Their vernacular languages have long
ago become the vehicle for their thought and their literature.

In our times, those writers on Islam who would write in
Arabic might reach, and be known in, the whole Arab-speaking
world and those non-Arab Muslims who have knowledge of that
language. But even the various Arab nations have developed
their own favourite representative and celebrated writers. The
Iranians use their native Persian tongue; their works will be
read, outside their own country, by the Muslims of Afghanistan,
India and Pakistan who cherish Persian culture almost as their
own. Urdu, the principal language of Pakistan, is not understood outside the Indo-Pakistan subcontinent. The Indonesians
and other Far Eastern Muslims are even more remote from the
main stream of Muslim literary life; they had hardly any contact with the literary interests of western Islam, apart from the
religious ideas that emanated from the Azhar.

EPILOGUE

East Versus West—
Or Meeting of East and West?

I.

Thus, the Muslim world in the twentieth century has become one of the most fascinating societies to observe; from the western point of view, understanding the motivations of its actions and intellectual movements has become a necessity. Since World War II, it has been driven by dynamic forces such as it had not known since the early Middle Ages. Their repercussions are obvious in the political domain, but no less powerful in the intellectual and spiritual sphere.

In the first few centuries of its existence, Islam had been forced to exert its creativity in order to establish its social organization and to find the philosophic fundaments for its religious doctrines. Sporadically, in later centuries, men of genius rose within Islam, such as al-Ghazâlî, who re-examined its tenets and their justifications and thereby heightened its meaning for the Believers and endowed it with new strength for centuries to come. But the long period of stagnation followed, devoid of creative speculative re-investigation, that ended only in the nineteenth century with the intrusion of the West into the world of Islam.

The clash between the two cultures caused the modern Muslim to look at his faith and at himself with a critical eye, not entirely of his own volition, but because of the non-Muslims' criticism of his stand. He could no longer afford blindly to pursue his ancient mode of thought and of life, but had to embark on a process of introspection and self-examination. This search for the intrinsic values of Islam and for a justification of its religious ideas, as compared with the western outlook, is characteristic of present-day Muslim thought everywhere.

To undertake such honest self-appraisal is not without painful aspects for the Muslim; but there can be no doubt about its sincerity. Western scholars have levelled much criticism against the manner in which it has been undertaken. Muslim apologists have been accused of closing their eyes against the contradictions within the Islamic system, of begging the question and of being reluctant to re-investigate the bases for their faith. They have been charged with believing *a priori* in its pre-eminence and that of their Prophet and in the truth of their Revelation. But would men of other faiths easily concede that their creeds might not be true and that their doctrines could not stand up to rational criticism? or might they not claim, too, that religious faith is beyond rationalistic analysis?

The Muslim's position is aggravated by his being forced to examine his faith within its own frame of reference and, simultaneously, to assess its validity against ideas deeply alien to his own. Eastern and western mentality differ in spite of certain common traits. But the development of modern times have increased mental and physical contacts between East and West; therefore, the comparative value of their concepts for the two cultures and their mutual relations will now commonly, though not always rightly, be appraised by identical standards.

The material benefit that resulted for the West from its rationalism, its science and its technology, roused the Muslim's desire to participate in them. He tried to achieve that end by adjusting his own life to that of the West and by adopting some of its outer forms. But he found that the change was not as beneficial as he had hoped. The new ways did not fit in with his own cherished customs and destroyed values inherent (or thought to be inherent) in the "old-fashioned" life. Thus disappointed, he began to accuse the West of "materialism" and to extol the "spirituality" of the East as superior, deeper and more in tune with its real mind. This contrast was emphasized by many Muslim authors, even by Iqbâl and others of high standard; it became the stereotype accusation of less courageous or more biased writers. But this condemnation should not exhaust their inquiry, though it might serve as a start for an investigation into the contrast between the two cultures. At best, it may be an explanation, possibly an excuse, for past failures; but it can no longer be accepted as an alibi for all future inadequacies either by the West or by those Muslims who earnestly think of the necessity for adjustment, change and progress. Moreover, this definition of the conflict is inaccurate. The material progress in the West has nothing to do with its spiritual attitudes; the West is neither less nor more "spiritual" because of its material prosperity, nor would the East be forced to give up its "spirituality" in order to improve its material standards. In that context, the two terms do not belong to the same semantic category and cannot be thus contrasted or compared.

As in every movement, explanations of the position in the past are as necessary as carefully considered, forward-looking deviations from long-accepted routine. The present generation of Muslims is actively engaged in this revolutionary process; but they have yet to reach definite conclusions.

The essence of the conflict between modernism and the retrospective, conservative school of thought is the failure of the latter to understand the true character of change. The present essay has attempted to show that the concept of change and evolution had been a basic function within Islam itself in its early, formative period. Iqbâl found it inherent in the Koran itself and can therefore be called to witness by those who strive for progress by evolution. "The universe, according to the Quran, is liable to increase. It is a growing universe and not an already completed product which left the hand of its Maker ages ago, and is now lying stretched in space as a dead mass of matter to which time does nothing, and consequently is nothing" (p. 55). "Change, therefore, in the sense of a movement from an imperfect to a relatively perfect state, or *vice versa,* is obviously inapplicable to His life. But change in this sense is not the only possible form of life. A deeper insight into our conscious experience shows that beneath the appearance of serial duration is true duration. The Ultimate Ego exists in pure duration wherein change ceases to be a succession of varying attitudes and reveals its true character as continuous creation 'untouched by weariness' and unseizable 'by slumber or sleep' " (p. 59f.). Neither Muhammad 'Abduh who first broached the idea of "identity in change," nor Iqbâl who projected it forcefully, was condemned by his fellow Believers. On the contrary, both are revered in their own countries and beyond; their name is pronounced and their memory invoked with pride, awe and a touch of the reverence felt for sanctity. Iqbâl's tomb in the grounds of the Shahi Mosque in Lahore is already acquiring the atmosphere of a shrine.

II.

It may be asserted that Islamic development did not altogether stop when the "door of free investigation" had been closed after only a few centuries. True, the Canon was definitely established, but Muslim life continued to expand, and with it, the problems posed to its scholars, theologians, philosophers and jurists. It is significant that Ibn Taimîyah (1263-1328) had to demand the return to pristine Islamic concepts unadulterated by the innovations that had accrued to it. But such protest implied that there had been change and growth. The Wahhâbîs since the late eighteenth century felt impelled to reiterate Ibn Taimîyah's protest. Thus, though the new customs were formally ignored by Canon Law and Tradition, and attacked by zealots, Islam did not stop developing new forms and producing creative thinkers: al-Ghazâlî, too, the Reviver of the Faith through Sûfism, lived long after the closing of that gate.

It is therefore not sufficient, for a real understanding of the creative development of Islam, to search for the evidence of its intellectual growth only in the essays of learned men, whether conservative or progressive. Life itself takes a hand and forces people and communities to change their ideas and habits according to circumstances. Men want to improve their conditions; they will thus act towards achieving that goal first and search for a justification of their actions afterwards. By the time a learned conservative scholar would declare these innovations out of harmony with traditional custom or contrary to Muslim law, they would have established a place for themselves in the habitual pattern of the people and would find defenders as well as detractors. That has happened over and over again in Islam.

In our times, the cultural factors are not the only ones to produce the internal and outer restiveness of the Muslim, and generally the Asian, world. The pressures in the political field, owing to the redistribution of power and the levelling off of the preponderance of the West over the East, are inextricably interwoven with the latter's cultural revival. The greater the gain in cultural strength, the stronger becomes the political pressure and *vice versa*.

Westernization is therefore most obvious in the field of political and international relations, for adaptation to western modes of thought and practice in those spheres is comparatively easy. No religious inhibitions and prohibitions prevent the awakening Muslim nations from making full use of any device in the political game; the leaders may therefore borrow the techniques of national and international debate freely and without hindrance from any orthodox quarter. Furthermore, certain features of Islamic political theory can easily be applied to the contemporary political situation, e.g., the term *Jihâd* "Holy War" or the concept of Democracy.

Especially the latter term is freely used nowadays and alleged to be an ancient Islamic principle. There is no denying that the Islamic religion does not know any distinction between men as human beings, and Islam, in that social sense, always was democratic. But in its western, political connotation, democracy is only just beginning to emerge in the Muslim world. Its characteristic features, e.g., participation of the individual in the running of community affairs, judgement of persons and policies on their merits, equality before the law, and responsibility of the leaders to the people are slowly beginning to be demanded and conceded.

Pakistan is comparatively far advanced in its acceptance of political, western-type democracy; Iraq and Indonesia have provided for it in their constitutions. In all official pronouncements of Pakistan's leaders, the principle of democracy, understood as a combination of its western and Islamic sense, has been stressed. Muhammad 'Alî Jinnah, as Qâ'id-i-A'zam, exhorted his nation in a solemn speech to the Constituent Assembly on August 11, 1947, to dedicate itself to the achievement of real democracy. Prime Minister Liaqat 'Alî, too, repeatedly stressed it in his addresses to the people of Pakistan and in lectures abroad. It found its culmination in the Pakistani Constitution which is a remarkably successful blend of indispensable principles of western democracy with the ideals of Islam. The test of their sincerity came in 1956 when, for the first time since Independence, the office of Prime Minister had to be turned over to a leader of the Opposition party. Viewed from the standpoint of Islam, that event may have been the first sign of a synthesis between the basic ideas of Islamic and western democracy: the responsibility of all for the common weal and the acceptance of the will of the majority as the guiding principle over that of the minority.

In other countries, as for instance, in Egypt, internal developments are delaying the emergence of democracy in the western sense despite some incipient trends. Nonetheless, in spite of various shortcomings, none of the Muslim nations can afford any longer to ignore the demands from their people for a share in the affairs of their nation. This desire has often been abused by politicians for their own purposes, witness the demonstrations by huge masses or by students and even school children that break out "spontaneously" whenever required. But a generation is being educated, many in the universities of the West, that will understand the true meaning of democracy. They will no longer be satisfied with being used by the parties or governments of the day, but will represent the real will and desire of the people.

III.

Somewhat paradoxically, in its defence against the encroachment of the West, the East is increasingly using the techniques and slogans that the former had taught it. President Wilson's "self determination of peoples" had awakened them to reconsider their national destiny; now that call is being turned into a weapon against the western nations to give moral support to the demands of subject people for independence. The Muslims ward off western accusations of callousness against their downtrodden masses by contrasting their ingrained respect for men of any colour with the western treatment of the Negro.

This is not a mere use of slogans. Centuries of exposure to western influence, ideological penetration and political and social domination have left their imprint on eastern thought and reactions. That is especially true in the social sphere. The western peoples endeavoured, with some measure of success, to eradicate illness, poverty and ignorance from their domains and to bridge over, at least in certain respects, the gulf between the upper classes and the masses. No contemporary ruler or government in any eastern land can afford to ignore the chasm that separates the comparatively few well-fed, educated rich from the multitudes of hungry, ill-clad, illiterate dispossessed people within its borders. With some justification, they could formerly put at least part of the blame for these conditions on their erstwhile conquerors. But since they have become masters in their own lands, they will have to bear the responsibility themselves. Muslims will have to acknowledge, too, that their ancient method of almsgiving is not sufficient, though it offers the Islamic state a good traditional basis for the introduction and justification of modern measures to eradicate poverty and to raise the standard of living of their people.

Thus, the external as well as the internal revolution, in the last analysis, is western inspired. Whether it is expressed as nationalism of an individual nation, or as a rally of Asians against the predominance of western power, the ideological fundaments and the methods employed—alliances, conferences, committees, negotiations—were learned under western tutelage.

That does not invalidate their right to self-assertion, however painful certain of its manifestations may be for their former tutors. Significantly, the guidance of mature, responsible leaders is increasingly effective in those countries that have enjoyed several years of consistent development, undisturbed by extreme internal or external upheavals, such as Iraq, India, Pakistan and, until recently, Indonesia. There the western political ideas became impregnated with indigenous concepts to form workable instruments for their new society. Liaqat 'Alî could proclaim with perfect sincerity, in a mass meeting in Lahore in 1949, that "For us there is only one ism—Islamic socialism, which in a nutshell means that every person in this land has equal rights to be provided with food, shelter, clothing, education and medical facilities. . . . The economic programme drawn up some 1,350 years back is still the best for us." By means of this simplification, he equated the western sociological theory with traditional Islamic practice, making his intentions clear to both western observers and his Muslim followers.

This is not merely a utilization of traditional habits and attitudes in order to make innovations and changes palatable to the Muslim masses; it is an attempt to imbue western-inspired ideas, the newly accepted values with the traditional emotions, to amalgamate them with the familiar pattern and to impart to them something of the sanction of ancient religious tradition.

IV.

In both East and West, the increasing Westernization of the former has often been regarded with some apprehension. The pace of its spread, in particular, has been criticized in both camps; the increasing adoption of less desirable facets, irreligiosity, superficial acceptance of western customs, misapplication of its slogans, was especially deplored. At the same time, western technology and production methods were being introduced at the insistence and with great financial and intellectual efforts of both sides. But when the results were not entirely commensurable with the hopes raised, disappointment and derision followed. Disillusioned western observers disparaged the superficiality of that Westernization and ridiculed certain extraneous manifestations that appeared to be only a veneer thinly covering ancient habits. Eastern circles, on the other hand, blamed the West for its failure to produce miracles, for falling short of expectations; it was accused of helping only for selfish reasons, of upsetting native habits and, last not least, of not doing enough.

In addition to such accusations in the material and technological field, the West was charged with upsetting the spiritual equilibrium of the East. For, though criticizing the haste with which traditional forms were discarded, it had attempted to teach the East either western rationalism or Christian doctrines and disregarded the reluctance of the East to give up its own stand. Thus contradictory charges and countercharges were proffered simultaneously on either side.

Yet, as in medieval Islam, western thought, when accepted, had not remained entirely unchanged. Modern philosophic ideas were passed through the sieve of Islamic faith and only those features that could be fitted into its mould were accepted. The western thinker was amazed at the transmutation that his thought had undergone in the process and at the "Orientalization" of his way of life in its eastern appearance. Through this subtle transformation even the "westernized" Muslim remains Oriental and his Westernization does not simply mirror his prototype. Such adaptation and selective assimilation takes place wherever different types of civilization meet and merge, for instance, in the "melting pot" of America.

Mutual understanding is, paradoxically, made more difficult by the fact that the ultimate roots of western thought and belief reach into the religious ideas of the Near East and Hellenism, the same soil from which Islam, too, had sprung. For that reason, Islam and Christianity, and even more, Islam and Judaism, are spiritually and intellectually very close; to that extent, the three religions do understand each other. But for the same reason, the western student of Islam, from his Judaeo-Christian and Hellenistic platform, expects it to conform to his own attitudes more than it does, more than it can do; for after all, it is neither Judaism nor Christianity, but Islam. The Jew or the Christian regrets its inability to reach, as he understands it, the spiritual height of his own religion. For the Christian, the insurmountable obstacle lies in the Muslim's repudiation of the Divinity of Christ, of the Trinity and of Jesus' Resurrection. The great stumbling stones for the Jew towards a deeper understanding of Islam are the Ka'bah and the rites of the Pilgrimage.

Conversely, the Muslim's strict conception of monotheism renders the Christian Trinity incomprehensible for him. "Say: He, Allâh, is One, Allâh is Eternal. He begetteth not nor was He begotten and there was none equal to Him." Though Islam considers Jesus as one in the line of Prophets from Moses to Muhammad, He is, in Muslim eyes, human, though, like them, the recipient of divine revelation. In medieval polemics between Jews or Christians and Muslims, these differences in belief were emphasized as criteria for the superiority or inferiority of their respective faiths. Some of these disputations, as reflected, for instance, in Judah Halevi's (1085-1140) al-Khazârî, reached high philosophic level, while others were mere mutual recrimination and slander. The Muslims insisted that the Jews ought to have acknowledged the Prophet and accepted his assertion that Koran and Torah were one and the same revelation, differing only in language, not in substance. The Prophet accused them in the Koran of falsifying their Scripture to avoid accepting him; he later excluded them from the Medinian Community of Islam. The Koranic attitude still determines the average Muslim's picture of Judaism and the Jews. Still, Jewish concepts are far more comprehensible to the Muslim than Christian doctrines, and the Jewish visitor to Muslim lands is cordially welcomed as one of the "People of the Book." Mutual understanding and sympathy is readily established between Jews and Muslims of any social or intellectual level.

Muslims themselves are increasingly pointing to the similarities between their beliefs and those of the two other monotheistic religions. In this manner, they are repudiating any possible implication of inferiority of their religion to Judaism and Christianity. That attempt harks back to the early Muslim commentators of the Koran and was continued in the medieval disputations.

For the western scholar, the reluctance of the Muslim intellectuals to accept the critical detachment of western research into the origins of religions is somewhat amazing. Comparative study of religions and analysis of the history of religious thought have accustomed the former to view solving such problems as a task of scholarly study rather than of faith. Their methods and results, however, are dismissed by orthodox Muslims as "western rationalism that contradicts the faith of the true Believer." Revelation, the divine origin of the Koran as the Word of Allâh, and the Prophet as His mouth-piece, are sacrosanct and any effort to interpret these traditional dogmas by means of modern scholarship is deemed inacceptable. At the most it is granted that acceptance of the traditional beliefs is a matter of faith "that defieth understanding." The Muslim is thus joining Jewish and Christian fundamentalists in this repudiation of rational analysis and sublimated or symbolic interpretation of basic doctrines.

The denial of western rationalism by otherwise westernized Muslims seems to be largely based on the fear that its acceptance might lead to abandoning Islam altogether. The intellectual and scientific thought of Muslim modernists may move in the realm of the most complicated, most advanced scholarship; but their scientific insight is hardly ever allowed to interfere with their faith. Well-known Jewish and Christian scholars established that same separation between their scholarly work and their religious belief. But for the Muslim this opens a wider chasm. For in the West, the divorce of the secular from the religious sphere has long been an accepted phenomenon, while for the Muslim the two remained intertwined.

The root of the conflict, however, is in a basic principle. The West justifies the need for a fresh search for Truth with every new insight and acknowledges that, though it is not variable itself, its comprehension is not unalterably established through revelation. By solving ever more of the problems posed by nature, science, though no handmaid of theology, serves to answer the religious questions as well. Scientific and religious search are born of the same fundamental urge; they inquire after the origin of the world, the laws that determine its continuance, the principles that govern its functions. In theological language, it is the quest for God, Creation, Life, Death, Resurrection; in scientific terms, it is the search for the laws that regulate the Universe in all its manifestations. Experimental and theoretical science throughout the centuries have brought us nearer to the solutions of these riddles. Kepler, Galilei, and Newton, in the past, Einstein in our own age, have explored it and discovered, each with the theoretical insights and the laboratory devices of his own age, many, though not yet all, of those laws.

In modern Islam, Muhammad Iqbâl unfortunately led the way to the flight into faith. When he delivered his *Lectures on the Reconstruction of Religious Thought in Islam* in Oxford, he added a seventh lecture to the original six. In it, he introduced "Higher Sûfism" as an escape from drawing the consequences of his own critical and daring reflections, and thereby weakened the impact of the six preceding, remarkably advanced and liberal, discourses. "It seems that the method of dealing with Reality by means of concepts is not at all a serious way of dealing with it. Science does not care whether its electron is a real entity or not. It may be a mere symbol, a mere convention. Religion, which is essentially a mode of actual living, is the only serious way of handling Reality. As a form of higher experience it is corrective of our concepts of philosophical theology or at least makes us suspicious of the purely rational process which forms these concepts. Science can afford to ignore metaphysics altogether . . . . but the religious expert . . . . cannot, in view of the final aim of his struggle, be satisfied with what science may regard as a vital lie, a mere "as-if" to regulate thought and conduct" (p. 184). In this way, Iqbâl returned to the ancient argument that scientific knowledge is incomplete and only religious experience that leads to religious certainty could encompass the whole. Already in an earlier lecture of the series he had claimed the same limitation for philosophy. "Philosophy is an intellectual view of things. . . . It sees Reality from a distance, as it were. Religion seeks a closer contact with Reality. The one is theory, the other is living experience, association, intimacy" (p. 61). By further demanding that man should rise to "a fresh vision of his origin and future, his whence and whither" by "religion which in its higher manifestations is neither dogma, nor priesthood, nor ritual [and which] can alone ethically prepare the modern man for the burden of the great responsibility which the advancement of modern science necessarily involves" (p. 189), he reinvested religion and faith with their ancient power of arbiters of all thought, insight and belief in Islam. Iqbâl's very greatness and his deep influence on the thought of the leaders of modern Pakistan make his hesitation particularly regrettable, for it may retard the intellectual development of his nation.

V.

Nonetheless, the comparatively high degree of similarity in their religious ideas facilitated, though it also aggravated, the intellectual contact between the western and the Islamic worlds throughout the ages. The latter had consistently exerted a deep attraction on the West that was partly romantic, partly born of greed for the "fabulous" riches, partly hostile, as in the Crusades. But the East was never for long entirely left out of western consciousness. From antiquity into modern times, travel, commerce and scholarship connected the two worlds; this interrelation was interrupted only for relatively short periods.

Since its re-emergence from such an interval of isolation, Islam must again integrate western currents of thought into its own pattern as it had to do throughout its history. But the West, too, is receiving new stimuli from the renewed participation of Islam in the intellectual processes of our age. If anywhere, there is cross-fertilization in the relation between Islam and the West. In the Middle Ages, the former had accepted Greek philosophy into its system of thought; however, its teachers were not unadulterated Aristotle and Plato, but the masters in their neo-Platonic garb. Near Eastern thought had, moreover, long ago penetrated into pre-classic Greece; it was re-introduced, via neo-Platonism, into Islam. This, and not classical Greece, entered the "monolithic bloc of Islam," as Louis Massignon stressed not long ago. Christian ideas with their admixture of Near Eastern and Hellenistic elements also entered into it.

In medieval philosophy, Islam returned the gifts that it had received from the West. Outstanding European philosophers, scientists and poets knew and perused the works of Muslim scholars and introduced their ideas into their systems; among them were Roger Bacon (died 1280), St. Thomas Aquinas (ca. 1227-1274), Raymundus Lullus (died 1315), Dante Alighieri (1265-1321). In more modern times, Daniel Defoe is said to have conceived his *Robinson Crusoe* under the influence of the philosophic romance *Hayy ibn Yaqzân* by the Spanish-Arab writer Ibn Tufayl (died 1185); its principal idea resembles also that of Rousseau's *Émile*. Generations of children and adults have been thrilled by the *Arabian Nights* ever since Galland's translation into French, the first into a European language, appeared in 1704. The strong mutual attraction is again apparent in our own age in human relations, art, literature, the dance and religious and philosophic trends.

There is thus a core of Oriental heritage in the western spirit, supplementing the Near Eastern origin of Christianity, that has created a receptivity for the spiritual values of the East and provided a common ground between Orient and Occident. Their discordances, other than political ones, on the other hand, were born of the difference in the mental experience of the two cultures in the two thousand years intervening between Jesus and the modern age.

The direction of the cross-fertilization between them changed from age to age throughout history; in recent times it had been predominantly from the West to the East. But a certain counter-current can already be detected; the turning of the tide in the flow of influences is setting in. After the eager acceptance of western modes, on their face value, as beneficial, the East is re-evaluating their contents and various aspects. It distinguishes several main roads of penetration. It is willing to accept whole-heartedly those influences that have entered into its pattern through technology; it may demand minor adjustments to avoid disturbing indigenous customs that have remained valid even under new conditions. Therefore, not only piecemeal techno-logical improvements, but the basic premises of modern indus-trialism and technology are accepted. There is no country in the East that has not been reconsidering its socio-economic out-look in their light. There is nothing in Islam that prohibits full utilization of every technical and scientific device; thus even the most advanced methods resulting from revolutionary dis-coveries in science may be used purposefully and without ob-struction from any quarter.

But in the intellectual, cultural and especially the religious sphere, the trend towards Westernization has been checked con-siderably. Western ideas are not totally denied acceptance, but indigenous religious and philosophic attitudes are emphasized, native expressions in art and literature furthered, native music and poetry cherished, native dance and dress propagandized, folk arts and crafts revived and supported. It is deeply significant for the whole trend that the escape from oppression for the Scheduled Classes, the so-called "Untouchables," in India is no longer sought in conversion to Christianity or Islam, but in Buddhism, an Asian religion not identified with the West or felt to be akin to it ideologically. It is even more striking that the leader in recent mass conversions to Buddhism should have been a western-educated scholar, the late B. R. Ambedkar (died 1956).

But it is equally significant that the two nations into which the Indo-Pakistan subcontinent was divided were both led by men who were "westernized" in the deepest and best sense of that term. Jawarhalal Nehru as well as Muhammad ʿAlî Jinnah were acknowledged and acclaimed as representing the deepest instincts of their peoples, not in spite, but possibly just because of their Westernization. Though having absorbed the analytical western approach, they appreciated and, consciously or sub-consciously, applied the spirit of synthesis inherent in the East.

They are a symbol for the possibility of a union between the western and eastern mentalities that will not result in a split personality, but a new personality, of the East.

VI.

In all these currents and countercurrents, our generation is witnessing a cultural revolution comparable to the most decisive epochs and turning points in the history of mankind. It is not only an entirely new distribution of political power—that statement is so obvious as to be almost trite—but the emergence of new emotional desires that the West and its culture alone cannot satisfy, not even for itself. For in spite of its seeming self-assurance, the West is no longer quite as certain about its own righteousness as it used to be. Ever since the explosion of the first atomic bomb, it has had severe misgivings about the direction in which it seemed to be going.

For that reason, personalities of the East are acquiring new meaning for the West regardless of their political stand, for, having assimilated western thought, they know the problems of the West, yet have remained "Asians." They thus represent not only the emotions and aspirations of Asia, but personify the tensions of our time and the hopes for the future of the whole world. Compared with his Indian counterpart, Muhammad 'Alî Jinnah is more difficult to understand in spite of Pandit Nehru's seemingly contradictory character. Nehru is more comprehensible to the West, for his complexity is not unexpected, as India herself is felt to be "mysterious" and "inscrutable." The similarity of Islam to western thought, on the other hand, leads the West to expect from a Muslim the familiar, the facile, the comprehensible; it is amazed when the unexpected, the unfamiliar, the incomprehensible happens.

There is thus no longer a one-sided process of assimilation of one side to the other, but a rapprochement between East and West. The distance both have travelled on the road to a meeting, in terms of international politics, can be measured by comparing the membership roster of the League of Nations and the problems before it, with those of the United Nations. Apart from the settlement of the succession to the Ottoman empire, which was concluded almost entirely with a view to European interests, the only Asian problem before the former was the "incident" between Japan and China into which the League refused to be drawn. Even the Emperor of Abyssinia appealed in vain for its help. In contrast, a large proportion of the problems confronting the United Nations have concerned Asia or Asian relations with the West. On the surface, much that happens in that continent seems to be directed against the West. But frequent pressures and apparent intransigence on either side do not hide the ever-growing realization that the world has, indeed, become one. The failure of the League of Nations to understand Asia's importance for the world was at least a major contributing factor in its demise.

There is furthermore a growing recognition that the concept of One World encompasses more than political cooperation. It demands the conviction that in spite of the varieties of races, colours, faiths and philosophies, there is unity in human suffering, dignity and destiny. Islam has always known and practiced this principle; within its wide realm, it sheltered widely different civilizations and peoples, within its religion, it harboured widely divergent attitudes. In the past, Islam had made western thought so much its own that the Muslims almost forgot its foreign origin and felt it to be genuine Islam. It will also gradually integrate the western ideas that it has absorbed more recently into its cultural pattern, and later generations will hardly be aware of their western parentage. At no stage of Islamic development did it matter whence its ideologies came. Their credentials were considered satisfactory when they proved compatible with the tenets of Islam. The quest of the western Orientalist for the origin of Koranic ideas is, to the orthodox Muslim, rank heresy, while later foreign intrusions got authoritative approval and became "Islam," or else, were refused acceptance by the same authorities. Whatever was accepted, was assimilated thoroughly and refashioned in Islam's own image; the result was the integrated *Weltanschauung* that is Islam.

Westernization as such, therefore, need not be viewed with

alarm. In itself, it is neither good nor bad; it is not even an indispensable condition for a better understanding between Islam and the West or for its own improvement and progress. A fresh approach to, and a new interpretation of, its own tenets in harmony with the demands of a more closely interrelated world would render many of its facets as valid for today as they had been in the past. East and West need not be, are not, antagonistic; they are complementary. Their hostility towards each other had its root primarily in political or economic, not in spiritual differences, though the latter often served as a pretext.

But because both are involved in that problem, it is necessary that they understand each other's motives and idioms. Mutual understanding may be more easily established with Islam than with non-Muslim Asia, for, as far as religion is concerned, they speak a closely related, though not an identical, language. The political rivalries and antagonisms loom large in their day-by-day relations; but they shift, improve or deteriorate with the constellations of power politics and the pressures of real or alleged national interests. They may help or hinder the progress of real understanding on the human and spiritual level; but the political alignments as such are not decisive. East and West alike must aspire to understand each other's inner motivations. But that presupposes mutual sympathy and emotional response to the other's spirit.

The East is forcefully demanding such understanding from the West. Any book published, any statement made by public figures or private individuals, is scrutinized for this spiritual sympathy. The retelling of an anecdote about the Prophet, even though taken from an ancient venerated Muslim source, will rightly rouse the Muslims' ire if it reveals lack of that sympathy. But the West, too, must expect from the East a better understanding of its motives and spiritual well-springs. The American visitor in Muslim lands is frequently shocked and hurt by misstatements about his society and judgements of its ways based on distorted reports. Indeed, while American intellectuals are searching honestly for the soul of the East, their eastern counterparts are too often satisfied with sweeping generalities about the American way of life. Judgements are often superficial, frequently based on outmoded authorities; passing fads are taken seriously as representative customs. Examples are too numerous to need citing, and every serious student or casual traveller in eastern lands can easily contribute instances from personal experience.

Understanding cannot be one-sided. But though the West is justified in its demand for honest appreciation of its own motives, it must be patient. For the East, whether Muslim or other, is passing through a most critical period of searching for its own soul and of adjustment to a modern world that is no longer spacious enough for people to live according to their own pattern, regardless of close neighbours or distant friends. In the secular sphere, in politics, commerce and scholarship, interaction, in spite of adversities and setbacks, is comparatively close. Despite many clouds, all nations desire peace and search for it intensely, though harsh words are still too often heard and bellicose acts committed. The task of understanding the soul of our Eastern friends and their spiritual life, is delicate and requires sensitivity, charity, and tact.

The process of adjustment to this new, more confined, world is still in progress in East and West alike. The latter, at present, can only observe, rarely suggest solutions, though sometimes help in overcoming obstacles. It should, however, refrain from belittling or interfering, for selfish reasons, in the efforts made by the East towards its goal of finding its place in the ranks of mankind without losing its own identity and its soul.

Bibliography

ADAMS, Charles C., *Islam and Modernism in Egypt*. London. 1933.

ALBRIGHT, William F., *From the Stone Age to Christianity. Monotheism and the Historical Process*. Baltimore, 1946. (The quotation on page 60 above is taken from page 231 f.)

ALI, A. Yusuf, *See* KORAN

AMBEDKAR, B. R., *Pakistan, or the Partition of India*. 3rd edition, Bombay, 1946. (The quotation on page 164 above is taken from page 13.)

ARAB HERITAGE, The, edited by Nabih Amin Faris. Princeton, 1944.

AL-ASH'ARI, *Al-Ibânah 'an Usûl ad-Diyânah* (*The Elucidation of Islâm's Foundation*). A Translation with Introduction and Notes by Walter C. Klein. Philadelphia, 1940. (American Oriental Series, vol. XIX.)

BECKER, Carl H., *Islamstudien. Vom Wesen und Werden der Islamischen Welt*. 2 vols. Leipzig, 1924, 1932.

BIRDWOOD, Lord, *India and Pakistan. A Continent Decides*. New York, (1954).

BROWN, W. Norman, *The United States and India and Pakistan*. Cambridge, Mass., 1953. (The American Foreign Policy Library.)

COON, Carleton S., *Caravan. The Story of the Middle East*. New York, 1951.

DIETERICI, F., *see* AL-FARABI.

DONALDSON, D. M., *The Shi'ite Religion*. London, 1953.

EDIB, Halide, *Conflict of East and West in Turkey*. (Jamia Millia Extension Lectures, 1935.) Lahore, s.a.

AL-FARABI, *Die Staatsleitung von Alfarabi. Eine Metaphysische und ethisch-politische Studie eines Arabischen Philosophen* . . [by] Friedrich Dieterici. Herausg. . . . von P. Brönnle. Leiden, 1904.

—————, *Der Musterstaat des Alfarabi* [trsl. by] F. Dieterici. Leiden, 1900.

FISCHEL, Walter J., *Jews in the Economic and Political Life of Medieval Islam*. London, 1937. (Royal Asiatic Society Monographs, XXII.)

FRANKFORT, Henri, *The Birth of Civilization in the Near East*. Bloomington, Ind., 1951. (The quotation on page 70 above is taken from page 16.)

——————, *Kingship and the Gods. A Study of Ancient Near Eastern Religion as the Integration of Society & Nature*. Chicago, 1948. (An Oriental Institute Essay.) (The quotations on pages 80-81 above are taken from page 278.)

FYZEE, Asaf A. A., *Outlines of Muhammadan Law*. Oxford, 1949.

GAUDEFROY-DENOMBYNES, Maurice, *Muslim Institutions*. Translated from the French by John P. McGregor. London, 1950.

AL-GHAZALI, *see* SMITH, M.

GIBB, H. A. R., *Modern Trends in Islam*. Chicago, 1947. (The Haskell Lectures in Comparative Religion . . . 1945.)

GIBB, H. A. R., and BOWEN, Harold, *Islamic Society and the West. A Study of the Impact of Western Civilization on Moslem Culture in the Near East*. 2 vols. Oxford, 1950, 1957. (vol. I, page 30-31 quoted above on page 89.)

GOLDZIHER, Ignaz, *Muhammedanische Studien*. 2 vols. Halle, 1889-90.

——————, *Vorlesungen über den Islam*. Heidelberg, 1910.

GRUNEBAUM, Gustave E. von, *Medieval Islam. A Study in Cultural Orientation*. Chicago, 1946. (An Oriental Institute Essay.)

GUILLAUME, Alfred, *The Traditions of Islam*. Oxford, 1924.

——————, *Islam*. Harmondsworth, 1954.

HAIKAL, Muhammad Husain, *Hayât Muhammad*. 4th edition, Cairo, 1947.

HAMIDULLAH, Muhammad, *The Muslim Conduct of State*. Lahore, 1953.

HITTI, Philip K., *History of the Arabs*. 3rd revised edition, London, 1946 (also later editions).

HOROVITZ, Joseph, *Indien unter Britischer Herrschaft*. Leipzig-Berlin, 1928. (Handbuch der Englisch-Amerikanischen Kultur.)

——————, *Koranische Untersuchungen*. Leipzig-Berlin, 1926.

HOURANI, A. H., *Minorities in the Arab World*. Oxford, 1947.

——————, *Syria and Lebanon. A Political Essay*. London, 1946.

HUSAIN, Taha, *Al-Aiyâm.* 2 vols. Cairo, s.a.

—————, *Idem,* English Translation: Part 1: *An Egyptian Childhood,* translated by E. H. Paxton, London, 1932; Part 2: *The Stream of Days,* translated by H. Wayment, Cairo, 1943.

—————, *Mustaqbil al-Thaqâfa fî Misr.* 2 vols. Cairo, 1938.

—————, *Idem,* English Translation: *The Future of Culture in Egypt,* translated by S. Glazer. Washington, D.C., 1954. (Near Eastern Translation Series, no. 9.)

IBN KHALDUN, 'Abd ar-Rahmân, *al-Muqaddimah. Prolégomènes.* Texte arabe par Quatremère. 3 vols. Paris, 1858. (Notices et Extraits des Manuscrits de la Bibliothèque Impériale, XVI, 1; XVII, 1; XVIII, 1.)

—————, *The Muqaddimah. An Introduction to History.* Translated from the Arabic by Franz Rosenthal. New York, 1958. (Bollingen Series, XLIII.)

—————, ISSAWI, Charles, *An Arab Philosophy of History. Selections from the Prolegomena of Ibn Khaldun of Tunis (1332-1406).* London, (1950). (Wisdom of the East Series.)

IQBAL, Sir Muhammad, *The Reconstruction of Religious Thought in Islam.* Lahore, 1954 (reprint; first published, Lahore, 1930, revised edition, London-Oxford, 1934). (The quotations in the text are taken from the 1954 edition.)

—————, *The Secrets of the Self (Asrâr-i-Khudi). A Philosophical Poem.* Translated from the Original Persian, with Introduction and Notes by Reynold A. Nicholson. 4th edition. Lahore, 1950.

—————, *Iqbal as a Thinker. (Essays by Eminent Scholars.)* Lahore, 1952.

ISSAWI, Charles, *see* IBN KHALDUN.

KLEIN, Walter C., *see* AL-ASH'ARI.

KORAN, The, *The Holy Qur-an.* Text, Translation and Commentary by Abdullah Yusuf Ali. 2 vols. New York, 1946.

—————, *The Koran (Qur'ân).* Translated by E. H. Palmer. With an Introduction by R. A. Nicholson. Oxford, s.a. (The World's Classics.) (The quotation on page 146 above is taken from A. Y. Ali's commentary, vol. 1, page 111; the numbering of Koranic verses follows Flügel's edition of the Arabic text.)

LEGACY OF ISLAM, edited by Alfred Guillaume and Sir Thomas Arnold. Oxford, 1931.

LEGACY OF ISRAEL, edited by Edwyn R. Bevan & Charles Singer. Oxford, 1948.

LEVI DELLA VIDA, Giorgio, *Les Sémites et leur rôle dans l'histoire religieuse.* Paris, 1938. (Musée Guimet, Annales. Bibliothèque de Vulgarisation, t. LIII.)

LEWIS, Bernard, *The Origins of Ismâ'îlism. A Study of the Historical Background of the Fâtimid Caliphate.* Cambridge, 1940.

LICHTENSTADTER, Ilse, "An Arab-Egyptian Family," in: *The Middle East Journal,* vol. VI. Washington, 1952.

—————, "The Muslim Woman in Transition," in *Sociologus,* N.S., vol. VII, Berlin, 1957.

—————, "From Particularism to Unity: Race, Nationality and Minorities in the Early Islamic Empire," in: *Islamic Culture,* Hyderabad, 1949.

LYALL, Sir Charles, *Translations of Ancient Arabic Poetry,* New York, 1930.

MANN, Jacob, *The Jews in Egypt and Palestine under the Fâtimid Caliphs.* 2 vols. London, 1920.

MARX, Alexander, *Essays in Jewish Biography.* Philadelphia, 1947.

MUSIL, Aloys, *The Manners and Customs of the Rwala Bedouins.* New York, 1928. (American Geographical Society, Oriental Explorations and Studies, vol. VI.)

NICHOLSON, Reynold A., *A Literary History of the Arabs.* London, 1907.

—————, see also IQBAL, M.; KORAN.

NOELDEKE, Theodor; SCHWALLY, Friedrich, *Geschichte des Qorâns.* 2nd edition. 2 vols. Leipzig, 1909, 1919.

QURESHI, Ishtiaq H., *The Pakistan Way of Life.* New York, 1956.

Report of the Court of Inquiry constituted under Punjab Act II of 1954 to enquire into the Punjab Disturbances of 1953. Lahore, 1954.

ROSENTHAL, Franz, see IBN KHALDUN.

SCHACHT, Joseph, *The Origins of Muhammadan Jurisprudence.* Oxford, 1950.

SIDDIQI, M. Mazheruddin, *Women in Islam.* Lahore, 1952. (cf. page 126 above.)

SIDDIQI, M. Raziuddin, "Iqbal and the Problem of Free Will," in: *Pakistan Quarterly,* vol. IV, Karachi, 1954.

—————, "Iqbal's Conception of Time and Space," in: *Iqbal*

as a Thinker, see IQBAL. (*See* page 23, quoted on page 188 above.)

SMITH, Margaret, al-Ghazâlî. London, 1944.

SMITH, W. Cantwell, *Islam in Modern History*. Princeton, 1957.

————————, *Modern Islam in India. A Social Analysis*. Lahore, 1942.

STERN, Gertrude H., *Marriage in Early Islam*. London, 1939. (Royal Asiatic Society, James G. Furlong Fund, vol. XVIII.)

SYMONDS, Richard, *The Making of Pakistan*. 3rd edition. London, 1951.

TOYNBEE, Arnold J., *A Study of History*. Abridgement by D. C. Somervell. Oxford, 1947. (The quotation on page 95 above is taken from page 488.)

ZINKIN, Maurice, *Asia and the West*. 2nd edition. London, 1953.

Index

minorities in: 92
see also: Yathrib
Minorities,
in Charter of Medînah: 58, 92
in Pakistan: 69, 151
see also: Pakistan; State, Islamic
status of—in medieval times: 90-3
religious minorities in Christian world: 91
integration of: 90-1
in Canon Law: 91-93
"Treaty of Protection": 90-3
integral constituents of Muslim empire: 91-92
in Muslim society: 92-93
hostility against: 93
could retain their faith: 94-95
non-Muslims in modern Islamic state: 151, 158, 163-64
in Egypt: 159
in Iraq, Iran: 164
Modernism,
part II, chapt. IV; epilogue;
passim;
position of women and—: 125-28, 130-33, 162
'Abduh and—: 161, 181
Iqbâl and—: 181
origin of: 180
no denial of Muslim doctrines in: 181
in literature: 191-92
see also: Education; Islam, Reappraisal of; Islam, Western Criticism of; Islam, Western Thought in; Westernization
Moneylender (*sarrâf*), 145
Monogamy, *see*: Polygamy
Monotheism, 53, 204
Moses, 204
"Mudar," 168
Muhammad 'Alî, Khedive, 169, 180
Muhammad (The Prophet),
passim;
character of: 42
his social conscience: 48, 85-86
his monotheism: 53
his religious development: 54-57
in Medînah: 57-59
as political leader: 56-58, 59-62

his position in later Islam: 59-62
in *Sunnah* and *Shî'ah*: 62
his view of prophetic office: 61, 88
his Leave-taking Sermon: 61
succession to: 61
"Seal of Prophets": 68, 86
his embassies: 71
unaware of power of Islam: 71
not a law-giver: 71-72
his actions as ideal: 72
his social ideas: 85-87, 144-46, 147-49
legislation on women: 123-24
preference for monogamy: 124, 130
economic ideas: 144
his "Night Journey": 172, 185
Muharram, see: Festivals
Muslim Brotherhood, The, 167-68
Muslims,
passim;
distinctive characteristics among Muslims: 168-69
self-appraisal of: 196
Mu'tazilah, The, 83, 98-101, 102, 103, 104

Nabî, 59-60
"Nâsikh and Mansûkh," 7-8, 98
Nationalism, 164-77;
diversity of races: 165
—and Pan-Islamism: 165-66
—and Pan-Arabism: 166-67
—and Arab League: 167-68
ancient antagonisms prevent Arab—: 168
—and racial origins: 169
versus Islamism: 170-4
Eastern and Western—: 170-1
see also: Nationality; Sukarno
Nationality, 168-69, 170-1
Near, Middle, East, 171;
nations developing in: 171
Nehru, Jawarhalal, 209, 210
Neo-Platonism, 101, 155-57
Newton, Isaac, 206
New York, 142
Nineveh, 169
Nizâm al-Mulk, 180
Nizâmîyah Academy, 103, 180